Think Yourself into Becoming a Language Learning Super Star!

Betty Lou Leaver, Ph.D.

Copyright 2019 by MSI Press, LLC
All rights reserved. No part of this book may be reproduced or utilized in any form or by any means, electronic or mechanical, including photocopying, recording, or by any information storage and retrieval system, without permission in writing from the publisher.

For information, contact
MSI Press
1760-F Airline Highway, #203
Hollister, CA 95023

Cover designed by Carl Leaver
Cover Graphic: Shutter Stock

Library of Congress Control Number 2019941991

ISBN: 978-1-933455-54-9

Contents

Acknowledgments 1

Introduction 7

Good Health Begets Good Learning 13

    Food: Eating for Good Grades 17

    Sleep 21

    Exercise 25

    Chemicals 29

Managing and Massaging Memory 33

    How Memory Works 37

    Awareness/attention 41

    Working Your Memory 43

    Time Off Marinating the Mind 55

    Remembering, Forgetting, and Lapses 59

Cognition 65

    All-or-Nothing Thinking 69

    Overgeneralization 73

    Mental Filtering 75

    Mustification 79

    Personalization 81

    Jumping to Conclusions 85

The Brainscape in Language Learning 89
Tolerance of Ambiguity 93
Ego Boundaries 97
Mental Management 99

Affective Dissonance 101
Emotional Reasoning 105
Self-Guidance 107
Disqualifying the Positive 109
Labeling and Mislabeling 113
Anxiety 117

Tactics and Strategies 121
Thinking Like a Good Language Learner 127
Tactics 129
Deepening Your Knowledge 133
Sharpening Your Skills 141
Making Errors 155

Individual Traits 159
Sensory Preferences 163
Personality Types 167
Cognitive Styles 175

Doing Well on Tests 183
Classroom Tests 187
Written General Proficiency Test 195

Oral Proficiency Interview (OPI) 199
Conclusion **203**
References & Resources 207
MSI Language & Culture Books 213
MSI Related Books 215

Betty Lou Leaver Ph.D.

Acknowledgments

Betty Lou Leaver Ph.D.

Ideas do not come out of nowhere. They come from experience, and, more important, they come from our interactions with others.

In composing this book, there are some interactions that have contributed greatly to how I view language learning and some people whose own ideas have greatly influenced mine in one or another way that is reflected in these pages.

The late Dr. Madeline Ehrman, long-time colleague, dating from when we worked together at the Foreign Service Institute (FSI), the teaching and training branch of the US Department of State, co-author, collaborator, and personal friend is ever present in many things I write today. Together, we worked through many student issues at FSI. She introduced me to Jungian personality type theory. I introduced her to cognitive styles. Together, we applied both concepts to student counseling. Later, we used what we learned from our students, our research, and our experiences with faculty development, which extended beyond the borders of the United States to more than 30 countries between us, to develop the E & L Cognitive Styles Construct, one of the topics in this book.

Another colleague at the Foreign Service Institute, Earl Stevick, whose book, *Memory, Meaning, and Method*

(2006) has influenced many language educators, became a long-term friend of both Dr. Ehrman and me. Earl's insight blessed all our professional discussions, and he helped me and others in numerous ways, including making the connection for me to an agent for brokering my first book contract. It was working extra hard with Earl (after his retirement!) on one problematic memory case that helped me develop a personal heuristic for problem solving in cases where students were not learning as fast as I felt they could.

Often, Dr. Ehrman and I joined forces with Dr. Rebecca Oxford, currently at the University of Alabama at Birmingham, who has made tremendous contributions to the field of Teaching English to Speakers of Other Languages and to language learning and teaching in general. We have published together, and we have networked together. Most important, though, many of the ideas in this book (and in our publications and presentations) have come from lively interaction that has fomented all sorts of new ideas, some that have initially been so far beyond the cutting edge that they were considered crazy until a few brave people led the way in incorporating them—and over time they became the status quo.

To the late Dr. Ekaterina Filatova, member of the faculty of the Department of Psychology at St. Petersburg State University, I owe an expanded understanding of personality types. Katya is revered as a preeminent leader in the establishment of socionics as a field of study in the Soviet Union/Russia. Attracted to her books on socionics, written in Russian, I became instrumental in seeing that her work was published in the United States, the seminal work, in fact: *Understanding the People around You*. When Katya died, I took over writing a series of companion volumes to her work. Each based on one of the 16 socions (four completed, 12 to go) and published under the pen name of Kacee Quinelle.

Dr. Maurice Funke, a brilliant applied linguist with whom I worked for many years at the Defense Language Institute Foreign Language Center (DLIFLC), whose work on cognitive distortions I have cited in this book, has always been at least a decade ahead of peers in understanding what needs to be brought into language programs, especially for and by students, to make programs successful. Dr. Funke's work has never been published, but it is well known to those of us who have worked with him. A generous colleague, he rarely asked for recognition and delivered worthwhile, insightful, and life-altering (at least, for language learning and teaching) ideas at the rate of a ball-pitching machine.

Dr. Shannon Salyer, currently with the Defense Manpower Data Center, has become my "partner in crime" in tackling issues of cognitive distortions and affective dissonances in language learning. Shannon and I worked together earlier at the DLIFLC for several years.

Another person with whom I worked at the DLIFLC, Youssef Carpenter, introduced me to the topic of mental management. He has successfully used mental management techniques with hundreds of military service members.

The late Boris Shekhtman, Una Cox Chapman Professor of Excellence at the FSI initially worked for me when I was the Russian Language Training Supervisor there. He worked almost entirely outside traditional approaches to language teaching, and everyone recognized his extraordinary talent at bringing students to very high levels of Russian language proficiency. Over the years, Boris and I became friends. He and I co-founded the Coalition for Distinguished Language Centers, an organization that focused on how to get learners to near-native levels of language proficiency. I copy-edited and published Boris's first book, *How to Improve Your Foreign Language Immediately* (currently published by Villa Magna LLC/edition 3), and I have shared the content of that book, with Boris's blessing, throughout the Eurasian world—and now here.

I cannot finish this list of individuals without including my own daughter, Dr. Echo Leaver, associate professor of cognitive neuroscience at Salisbury State University. They say that you teach your children when they are young, and once they are grown, they start teaching you. Echo's research on memory, especially memory and aging (no, I am not her subject!), has helped inform my work on memory in language learning. Additionally, two decades ago, we worked together on a predecessor to the E&L Cognitive Styles Construct. Hosted for a number of years on the website of the American Council of Teachers of Russian, the ALSAT (American Councils Learning Styles Assessment Test) served as the basis of the new test developed by Dr. Ehrman and me, known informally as the E&L.

Finally, I owe immense thanks to hundreds of teachers and thousands of learners I supervised over the years at FSI, DLI, NASA, and New York Institute of Technology-Amman (Jordan) as well as to even more hundreds of K-16 teachers and their students I advised and trained in more than 24 countries. To all these folks I owe an eternal debt of gratitude. I learned far more from them than I could possibly have taught them.

Introduction

Betty Lou Leaver Ph.D.

This is not your typical tip book on how to learn foreign languages. It does not tell you to do a list of 15 things and assure you that you will become the language classroom star. Such lists of tips do not work for all learners. Sometimes, almost none of the traditional tips and tricks work for some people.

This book does not offer you a comprehensive list of learning strategies for reading, listening, writing, speaking, memorizing for vocabulary, and getting good with grammar. There is no need for yet another book on the topic of learning strategies. Good books exist. The best on in opinion, is *Teaching and Researching language learning strategies: Self-regulation in Context* (Oxford, 2017). You should get it, use it, and keep it handy. You will not need a better guide for learning strategies than that. Oxford (1986) has also produced a well-vetted instrument: *Strategy Inventory for Language Learning.*

What this book offers

This book is different. While it does encompass some traditional tips that have usually worked for most people, including a significant number of learning strategies for developing reading, writing, listening, and speaking skills, acquiring vocabulary and grammar faster, and improving memory, and strategies, it mostly focuses on you, who you are, how you learn, and what you, personally, can do to make your learning easier, faster, and more fun. Most important, it is about how you think and how changing your thinking can help you become a much better language learner nearly overnight.

You are not some average Joe. You are a special, unique person with specific strengths and particular weaknesses. The source of your strengths can be maximized if you can identify the source and know how to maximize what is working for you. Likewise, you can minimize your weaknesses if you know what is not working for you and what might work instead. That is the point of this book: developing your own heuristic for successful language learning.

Who wrote this book

So, who am I to write this book? I have taught hundreds of students as a teacher of Russian and ESL. As an academic administrator, the focus of most of my career, I have overseen dozens of language programs, thousands of teachers (literally), and tens of thousands of students (again, literally). I have overseen US government programs for three government institutions (Foreign Service Institute, NASA, and Defense Language Institute) as well as for universities, for-profit institutes, and non-profit organizations.

Maybe even more important, I am and always have been a language learner. What I suggest in this book is a sharing of both what I have done as a successful language learner and also what I have seen as an administrator of language programs. As a language learner, I have been tested at near-native levels in French and Russian, professional levels in German and Spanish, and (estimated by a proficiency tester) a working level in Czech. In total, I have studied 19 languages. For a couple languages (Portuguese and Pashto), I had only a few weeks of familiarization with the language before having to use it formally in a country where it was the official language. So, in short, I think it is safe to assume that I know whereof I speak.

This experience has provided me with shortcuts and easier ways to learn languages. I have watched many students struggle unnecessarily and hope that you will not be one of them, thanks to this book.

How this book is structured

It can be difficult to divide the kinds of information in this book into neat little compartments of information because whatever categories one might use, they will overlap. For example, chemicals affect health, and health itself affects memory. Metacognitive strategies can help improve health but are probably more important for how they can help improve cognition and choice of cognitive strategies (for reading, listening, speaking, etc.).

The book starts with health because without good health you cannot learn well. It proceeds to discuss memory because memory is the basis of all aspects of language acquisition. From there, the topics move from generalized to personalized, ending with a topic we all might want to avoid but must address: testing.

Betty Lou Leaver Ph.D.

Good Health Begets Good Learning

Betty Lou Leaver Ph.D.

As mentioned in the introduction to this book, I introduced the section on health first. Without good health, there cannot be maximal learning.

Bodies that are hungry, trying to digest food at the same time that a learner sits down to study, or are full of junk food that does nourish the brain do not allow the brain to work at its maximum efficiency. Learning slows down. Put the right food in the body, and energy improves, memory improves, and language learning performance improves. Yes, food matters.

Sleep matters, too. Learners who doze off in class, fall asleep while studying, or otherwise are tired are working on half-thruster. They cannot take in new information efficiently. They cannot even use what they do know well.

Then, there is sloth. No one uses that word nowadays, but it is a good word. Learners who spend their time glued to a chair, couch, or bed will find themselves fighting fatigue—from doing too little. Get up, get out. Run. Go to the gym. Do whatever it takes to get the blood circulating in your body and the endorphins that come from exercising pumping through your veins. Those endorphins play an important role in learning.

Finally, watch out for chemicals. Our world is full of them. Some very innocuous ones are identified in the section on "Chemicals and Language Learning." They are not really innocuous, after all.

Here's to a healthy life style and a healthy language learning experience!

Food
Eating for Good Grades

At the Defense Language Institute (DLI) where I served as a provost for five years, I became known as the "banana provost" because I would encourage students to eat a banana daily and, for certain, to eat one on the morning of important tests. Why would I do that? Because of the role that bananas play in memory. Bananas contain potassium, which facilitates the movement of glucose through the brain. Glucose is important because it carries memory engrams.

eat a banana = remember more words

That formula may seem simplistic, but overall it works. Bananas are not the only foods, though, that carry potassium or that do good things for memory and learning. Others are listed below.

Good food for learning well every day

If you cannot stand bananas, then try some of these other foods that contain potassium and stabilize glucose:

potatoes	cantaloupe
honeydew	apricots
dried fruits	prunes
raisins	lime beans
pinto beans	kidney beans
soybeans	lentils

Eating one item from this list every day should help you remember those difficult words and grammar rules better.

Other foods can support learning in other ways. Look at the great choice you have:

- avocadoes increase blood to the brain
- fish, especially salmon, are great brain food (have some 2-3 times a week)
- blueberries are known to increase learning capacity in general (and they taste good)
- tea enhances memory, focus, and mood (a three-fer)

At the same time, avoid foods that make it more difficult to learn. Coffee, coke, candy bars, and other foods with caffeine may give you an immediate rush and sense of being more focused, but you will always crash when the caffeine wears off. With that crash comes greater difficulty remembering either new or old information.

good food = good brain

Food for that big test day

Test days demand physical energy and endurance and a brain working at its best, especially your memory. Those foods that are good to avoid on a daily basis are especially important to avoid on a test day. The last thing you want to happen is to have your brain go to sleep in the middle of a test because of an energy crash. Stick with the banana and add a carb, such as a bagel, for longer lasting nutrition and energy throughout the length of the test.

banana & bagel = best test

Of course, food won't magically produce good grades. You do have to study and prepare!

Bon appetit!

Betty Lou Leaver Ph.D.

Sleep

If you want to do well in your language courses, go to sleep. No, I am not talking about sleeping with a tape recorder under your pillow, quietly drilling language words into your subconscious. I am talking about getting a good night's sleep so that you can come to class awake and alert and have enough energy to get through tests without falling asleep. If good food gives your body the fuel it needs to learn efficiently, then sleep keeps your body in good repair so that your brain runs smoothly.

fuel (good food) + maintenance (sleep) = a smooth ride

During sleep, cells are regenerated. We stress our cells when we are awake, and we need sleep time for repair. We all know that. We all have pulled all-nighters for one reason or another, get up groggy the next day, and do not function well. We are lucky if we even remember what we did that day, let alone what we learned.

Sleep and learn better

Falling asleep in class from a long night (not worth it, really) or zoning out and missing an explanation about an important grammar rule (or what is going to be on the test) makes learning inefficient, difficult, and mostly unsuccessful. To remember things, we have to be aware of their existence to begin with. When the brain is doing its utmost to doze off, it is not aware of very much, let alone the intricacies of some aspect of a foreign language. Being aware requires being awake!

Sleeping to remember better

Remembering anything while hung over from lack of sleep is very difficult. Taking a test on fumes just does not pan out well. Successful language learning requires remembering vocabulary, grammar, cultural idiosyncrasies, and much, much more. That requires a brain that has been refreshed and is working at maximum efficiency.

Equally important, the brain continues learning during sleep. Don't believe that? Test it out! Take a long list of vocabulary items, too many to learn on the spot, and spend 5-10 minutes trying to learn them before going to bed. Note down how many you can recall before falling asleep. When you wake up in the morning, try listing the words you remember. Compare the list from the night before and the morning after. See a difference? Most people do.

Sleeping to perform better

Language learning, in part, is a matter of critical thinking—figuring out how words, grammar, topics, and cultural views come together in the ways speakers of the target language express themselves. In this respect, learning to understand a language facilely is like putting together a jigsaw puzzle; you keep filling in the missing pieces. People with critical thinking skills, however, complete the puzzle faster because they know to quickly scan pieces for specific color, sizes, or shapes. This kind of critical thinking transfers to language learning, and it requires focus. Focus, in turn, requires being awake and aware, not tired and drifting into and out of sleep.

Sleeping to improve your language learning environment

Chances are, if you are in a language course, your teacher will give you tasks to complete in small groups. Students often learn better when they work together, but that working has to be amicable and goal-oriented. When learners are exhausted from lack of sleep, they can be cranky—and cranky learners do *not* work together well.

Sleeping for a good test score

Whether you are taking the awe-invoking Defense Language Proficiency Test, an Oral Proficiency Interview from your teacher or professional tester, or just a course final, don't cram. Sleep! There is nothing that you can learn in the last few hours before a test, but there is a lot you can forget if you are tired the next day. Remember:

$$great\ rest = great\ test$$

Sweet dreams!

Betty Lou Leaver Ph.D.

Exercise

When one is studying intensively, it might seem an unnecessarily waste of time to get up and exercise. In fact, in the act of perseverance (the internal push to keep going), much time can pass unnoticed. All work and no play, however, is…well, you know.

Exercise advantages the language learner in a number of ways:

- release of feel-good endorphins;
- boosting of brain activity; and
- retention of new skills in memory.

The question, then, is not if you should exercise but rather when, how long, and how. Therein lies a number of options that you can choose from, depending upon your personal schedule, needs, and interests.

Exercise to improve mood and energy

Any exercise that prompts the release of endorphins will improve mood and energy. Both will serve you well in the classroom as you work with others, and you may also gain additional energy for homework and self-study,

active learner = happy learner

Exercise to boost brain activity

Any movement has been found to boost brain activity, including something as simple as standing up. So, after a little time studying, stand up. Do it often. Stretch. Do some jumping jacks, squats, yoga, whatever suits your fancy. Just move!

Try some aerobics, either as a study break or once a day. Suggestion: make it the first thing in the day, and you won't "forget" or run out time for your aerobics. Aerobics help with memory and critical thinking; that is another reason to start the day with aerobics.

The common thinking among medical professionals is that a 15-minute workout will boost brain activity. What are some activities you can do?

- If you are just starting language study, count your steps in the target language wherever you go.
- Walk or jog while listening to a broadcast or other lesson.
- Review your notes from class while on the treadmill.
- Get and use YouTube videos in your target language for gymnastics, yoga, etc.
- Dance to a foreign band's YouTube video while singing along (you may need to track down the lyrics—and make sure you understand them.
- Spend time at a gym on a regular basis with a native speaker (and talk as time permits).
- If at the gym alone, count your repetitions in your target language, recite dialogues as you row, and talk to yourself in your target language as you use any of the machines.
- Get your own coach in your target language. Check out Runtastic's physical fitness coaching programs; one of them will count out pushups for you in your target language.
- Check for other physical fitness apps online in your target language.
- Switch your fitbit to your target language.

spend physical energy = gain more energy + smarts

Retention of new skills in memory

In terms of physical skills, exercising for 15 minutes after learning or practicing a new skill helps retain that new motor skill. Similarly, some K-12 language teachers have noticed that some students learn vocabulary faster and retain it longer when they learn it through bouncing balls or otherwise moving and talking at the same time.

move more = remember more

Keep moving!

Betty Lou Leaver Ph.D.

Chemicals

I once had a student who appeared unable to retain anything she was taught. Trying to figure out the cause, I gave her a series of learning styles test, which had odd results. I called her into my office and told her, "Either you answered the questions very strangely, or you have a storm in your head."

"I have a storm in my head," she said, which was not the response I had expected.

It turns out that she had been given some incorrect prescription medicine that had caused some temporary brain damage. With her permission, I spoke to her doctor, who told me that the medicine had caused damage to short-term memory that would, over time, dissipate.

In the meantime, she had to learn a new language, and language learning depends heavily on short-term memory. Together with Dr. Earl Stevick, a colleague, friend, and well-known linguist with a penchant for innovative applications from the field of psychology, we worked out a program that taught her mainly through her long-term memory. The plan created much work for teachers and student alike, but it was worth it. We all learned a lot about memory, and the student reached a professional level of language proficiency in the normal amount of time—44 weeks of Russian at the Foreign Service Institute.

What does this mean for the everyday language learner? Chemicals are unseen. Chemicals are everywhere, Chemicals can create unexpected barriers to language learning, (learning of any sort, or intake and recall in general).

We can only cover a few of the chemicals here. Do some Internet searches, or keep up some medical journals (especially those intended for public consumption), and you will learn many surprising and useful things.

Allergy medication

Surprised by that subhead? My daughter, a cognitive neuroscientist specializing in memory, floored me with this information. The latest research shows that allergy medication (well, actually, any antihistamine, e.g. Claritin) can reduce the effectiveness of acetylcholine activity neurons, which can negatively impact memory. In simpler words, using antihistamines can interfere with your ability to learn new words, grammar, and ideas. Oops!

For most people, perhaps this is not a serious problem. What are a few depressed memory neurons? Well, maybe it is a problem for everyone in one way or another, but for language learners especially this can be a real problem, maybe even the straw that breaks the camel's back if you are already struggling to learn the language. (If you are a super-duper language learner, you probably don't have to worry.)

Obviously, if you need to take allergy medication, you cannot stop doing so just because you are in a language class. So, there has to be another answer. What can you do to compensate for antihistamines?

Here are some suggestions for getting around this problem. They don't make matters better, but if they are not considered, they can make matters worse.

- Don't rely on rote memory. Rote memory is the form of memory most affected by antihistamines. Use, instead, other kinds of approaches, such as making associations between new words and ones you already know. Associations can be made with sounds, word formation, and general knowledge. Also, use deconstruction—pull the word apart to understand it better, and you will remember it better.

- Use all your senses. The more senses you use, the more "routes" you have to store and retrieve new information. Read and visualize. Listen and say. Write and act out. Use every muscle in your body: tongue, eyes, fingers, arms, whole body to encode and store new words.

- Maintain good brain health. All those things Mom always tried to get you to do become very important if you are trying to preserve as much memory capacity as you can. Eat your daily banana! The endorphins not only help mood, they also help memory. Sleep! A sleep-deprived brain has difficulty doing anything!!

compensate for chemicals
with good choices = improve chances to succeed

Your brain on nicotine

Studies have shown that while smoking, including inhaling second-hand smoke, impairs brain function, former smokers have better cognitive function than current smokers (Rowan, 2011). The remarkable information for learners is that if you quit smoking, you can improve how well your brain—and especially, memory—works.

Quit smoking = learn better

Other sources of chemicals

The environment contains many chemicals. Remember the lead scare? We no longer have lead-based paints. Remember the mercury scare? We no longer put mercury into some medicines. Remember the asbestos scare? We no longer use asbestos. The Internet is full of stories of environmental chemical concerns. Follow a few stories for a while, and avoid what is dangerous as best as you can.

All foods contain chemicals, too. Some are more dangerous than others. Remember the mercury scare again? Most people are now very cautious about eating certain kinds of fish, such as swordfish. So, make sure you are putting good chemicals into your body, not bad ones and know what to do if you have to ingest ones that might impair learning. The Internet can provide you with a surprising list of good and bad food chemicals.

If you are unsure of what medicines can do to impede your learning, what foods might take the place of medicines, what chemicals you might be ingesting unknowingly, talk to your doctor or, if you have one, your physical trainer. Don't be caught unawares.

forewarned = forearmed

Know your chemicals, and use/avoid them wisely!

Managing and Massaging Memory

Betty Lou Leaver Ph.D.

While we do not know everything there is to know about how memory works, we do know enough to help us to use our memory more wisely and to build it up for language learning.

First, it is important to realize that memory improves with use. So, use your memory every chance you get—and it does not need to be only for language study.

Second, it is important to know how to avoid harming your memory, as discussed in the previous chapter. It is equally important to know how to help your memory, also discussed in the previous chapter.

Third, it is important to understand the various stages that go into remembering something, from being aware of the information, to storing it for a short period of time and for a long period of time, to retrieving it. Knowing how memory works helps us to do things to make it work better.

Fourth, as discussed in the last chapter, maintain good health to maintain a good memory. Eat foods thank improve your memory (or keep it working at its finest), meditate, run, chew gum (yes, there is some evidence that this helps), and eat berries, Oh, and you can have that cup of coffee you need; it will help consolidate the things that your brain must do to remember new information. Just don't drink coffee right before a long exam because the caffeine high will disappear before the test is over, and then you are stuck.

With that knowledge, we can make the most of the time we have to commit information to memory. In fact, we can do that a lot more easily than is typically assumed.

How Memory Works

The actual way in which memory works can be quite complex. Explaining it can require an entire book, and entire books have been written on the topic. For a book on how memory works with foreign language learning, see, for example, Stevick's *Memory, Meaning, and Method.*

Kinds of memory

Broadly speaking, we have short-term memory (sometimes called working memory although a distinction is also sometimes made between short-term memory as storage and working memory as manipulation of the items going into storage) and long term memory (sometimes, called permanent memory although permanent memory is sometimes used to mean very long-term storage that is not subject to loss). That is an extreme oversimplification, but it gives a starting point for understanding memory.

We also have episodic memory (memory of events), sensory memory (things we felt or touched), procedural memory (motor activities), semantic memory (retaining ideas and concepts) and declarative or explicit memory (memory of facts and information). All these kinds of memory are important to language learning, even motor memory, in which writing or acting out words, dialogues, or role-plays can help you remember the various pieces of the language you will need to use in other contexts as you individualize your speech or try to understand broadcasts or newspapers..

How memory works (simplified)

The kinds of memory mentioned above are actually the stages we go through in trying to remember something. They have specific locations in the brain, not discussed here because unless you have frontal lobe damage or a malfunctioning hippocampus it does not matter to you, as a language learner, what the physiology actually is. The stages of memory, briefly and simplistically, are

- attention/awareness;
- repetition/rehearsal (for short-term storage);
- manipulation of information (in working memory, in preparation for moving it to long-term memory; and
- use, recall/retrieval, and re-storage to make information impervious to loss (long-term memory).

Test this process out. You will have to do it over time.

1. Find 5-10 words (open the dictionary and blindly pick, if you like) in either English or your foreign language that you do not know. Figure out what those words mean. Do that first on your own by using some of the techniques listed above. Then, ascertain your accuracy by asking someone or looking up the meaning in the dictionary or online. You have now accomplished the awareness step of memory.

2. Repeat these words to yourself several times. Do it out loud, and also do it silently. Write them out. Use them in a sentence. Do a search for them online and find each one used by three different authors (easier if you are at least at the intermediate level in your foreign language). You have now completed the repetition/rehearsal step for short-term storage. You can go on to business as usual for a day.

3. The next day, look at those three words and see if you remember them. Write down their definitions. Use them in a sentence. Find them online again—in at least three different places. You have now partially completed the manipulation of information step to begin moving the information into long-term memory.

Think Yourself into Becoming a Language Learning Super Star!

4. Repeat step #3 once a week for three weeks. Then, put the words on a list, without any other information: just a list of words. Put the list in a drawer, and put a note on your calendar to look at the list in three more weeks.

5. Three weeks have now passed. Look at your list. How many of these words do you remember? The ones you remember are now in your long-term memory. Whether they will stay there even longer term or near-permanently will depend upon future activities, some of which you may have no control over, such as naturally encountering those words in new environments or having to use them for one thing or another.

Know how memory works to make better use of it!

Betty Lou Leaver Ph.D.

Awareness/attention

Sometimes called attention, sometimes called awareness, the very first step to remember something is to know it is there: to observe it and to understand it. If you do not notice something, how can you remember it? Seriously.

For example, if someone were to ask you ten years from now to tell them the font used in this book or to describe the chair you were sitting on when you read it, chances are you will not be able to—because you did not pay attention to those things. Why should you have? They were not critical to your goal in reading the book. Likewise, if you want to remember vocabulary, grammar, a letter in another alphabet, or a sound that differs from English, you first must notice it. So, let's talk about how to "notice."

Words

Rather than trying to remember a word as a whole, try paying attention to components of the word. How many syllables are there? What does the word sound like? What are the pieces of the word (the root, i.e. the letters/sounds that give basic meaning, prefix, suffix)? Is there anything else unique about the word that you can associate with something you already know?

identifying word components = word-observant

Grammar

Look for patterns. Look for similarities to other languages you know—are there simple letter substitutions that regularly occur? Are there syllables or even whole words that are almost the same? (We call these cognates.) Does the word order differ from English? Consistently?

Meaningfully? That is important to know. Do the words have endings that have special meanings? Do these endings occur in patterns? Do the beginning of words have special patterns change meaning?

identifying grammar patterns = grammar-observant

Letters or characters

Pay attention to the shape of the letter. To help you 'see" the shape better, try tracing it, and then copying it. If your language uses an alphabet, are any of the letters similar to English? Or to Greek (you may know some Greek letters from math classes or fraternity/sorority activities).

*identifying the shape of letters
and characters = letter/character-observant*

Sounds

Ask your teacher to correct you when you do not say the sound correctly. Compare words that sound alike (e.g., *pin, bin*) to help sharpen your ear's ability to notice sound differences. You may need your teacher's help because it is difficult to notice and even to hear sounds in another language.

sharpening your ear = sound-observant

Always be ready to be aware!

Working Your Memory

As I write this book, I have been arguing with Alzheimer researchers for a few weeks about memory. The catalyst for the argument was a crowd-funded test being used in Alzheimer research that asks respondents to remember word pairs. The test presents 10-12 word pairs one after another, then asks you to recall as many as possible, and then gives you two more tries. The ability to do this supposedly declines significantly with age. The researchers want to test the DNA of the outliers (those who score exceedingly well or exceedingly poorly—don't take the test if you don't want to be contacted for your DNA!)

I learned all of the pairs on the first try, which, of course, does not correspond to my age group or any age group—and now the researchers are after my DNA. They should not be. In my opinion (which should count for something, at least; and who knows me better than I do?), it is not my DNA; it is my memory strategies. The researchers argue with me about that, but, as I have explained to them, I get paid to remember words!

Here's how you can max that research test and your vocabulary quizzes. The following suggestions take advantage of how memory works and help your memory work better.

Make rote memory your back-up, not your primary approach

In addition to rote memory—staring at vocabulary lists, using flash cards—two other methods are available for learners: associative memory and instant recognition (sometimes called "binding"). Both are more efficient and effective than rote memory.

Rote memory

Rote memory is what you learn without a whole lot of meaning attached. Just repetition. There may be much better ways to get it from short-term to long-term memory. Remember the poems and songs you memorized in school as a child? Maybe you did not know every word, but you were able to recite the poem or sing the song because you had practiced it so much. That is rote memory.

I can personally provide a couple of examples that show both the power and the weakness of a rote memory approach to learning. When I was a child, I learned to sing the song, *Rudolph, the Red-Nosed Reindeer*. The last line says, "you will go down in history." However, I heard the last line as "you go down and hear a story." Never mind that my version made no sense, I continued to sing it that way for nearly two decades—until my first child was born, I bought the sheet music to play the song for her on the piano and noticed the correct wording.

When you learn something by heart, within a specific context, without understanding the meaning attached to what you have learned, you can only use it in one situation. It does not become something that is really part of your language tool chest, so to speak. Here another personal example might make the matter clearer. As a Russian student, I learned the word, *tygach*. I had no idea what that really was. However, the dictionary told me, as did my textbook, that it was a prime mover. The only problem was that neither I nor any of my classmates knew what as prime mover was. Nonetheless, we always got a good grade on our tests, which in those days were often translation tasks, by just using the word *tygach* when asked to translate *prime mover* and vice versus. Nearly 15 years later, I was sitting on a plane and saw a prime mover push the plane away from the airport. At that moment, all the different contexts in which

I had encountered *tygach* came to mind. I think anyone will agree that 15 years to find out the real meaning of a word is too long a time. That aside, rote memory had given me only a way to use the word *tygach* in a very restricted environment—on a translation test. Rote memory is not an efficient way to learn, and skills begin to decline after the age of 15.

Associative memory

Associative memory forms the basis of most learning strategies. Associative memory is a matter of comparing (associating) new information with known information. That way, it gets attached to what you already know and is easier to store because there is something in the storage area for it to hang onto. The famed French psychologist Jean Piaget found that knowledge grows by chaining new information to old information in a process he termed *assimilation* (Piaget & Inhelder, 1971/2015). As these chains grow in length, a person becomes more knowledgeable.

Binding

Binding (the "ah-hah!" event) occurs when something is recognized on the basis of being partially known earlier or just absolutely makes sense. In both instances, very likely associative memory is at play, but there is an emotional element involved. When any discovery is made, a joyful moment is typical—regardless of what that discovery is. The same is true for cognition (Thagard & Aubie, 2008). Neural scientists tell us that binding occurs thanks to the interweaving of neural structures (Thagard & Stewart, 2010), the details of which I leave to the scientists among you—check it out in the medical journals.

associate & bind = fast and efficient

Use memory strategies

Memory strategies help you store and recall words, phrases, and knowledge of grammar without lots of repetition, enabling you to use these elements of language sooner and more fluidly. There are many kinds of strategies. Some are below, listed not in any particularly order. Need a good book full of great memory strategies? Check out Rebecca Oxford's *Teaching and Researching Language Learning Strategies*. The list below is just the tip of the iceberg of extant strategies—and you may be able to come with some that work for you that have not been listed in any manual.

- Organize your study
- Focus your attention
- Pace yourself
- Compare (associate)
- Make connections (use mnemonics)
- Use roots
- Structure
- Elaborate and rehearse
- Visualize concepts

Organize your study

Learning occurs more effectively and, really, more efficiently, when you have a plan for it. Break your semester into weeks, weeks into days, and days into tasks and goals. How much do you want to learn each day? (Daily learning is far more effective than cramming and learning via periodic bursts of energy.)

Have a time and a place for studying. Our bodies and brains associate learning with specific times and specific locations—and we learn better in those times and places.

Focus your attention

Having that time and place for studying facilitates your being able to focus your attention. Your brain subconsciously identifies the time and the place with calm and studying. Once you have yourself in this place, plan to concentrate on what you are studying.

Make sure that you will be alone at this time and place. Eliminate all distractions, like television, noise, and activities going on around you. (Well, that is the professional advice of the experts. However, there are learners—I am one of them—who not only can handle distractions but also find that distractions are helpful because they force them to pay intent attention to what they are doing in order to exclude the background against which they are studying. In college, I always made good grades, and I always did my studying in the dorm rec room. I cannot tell you for sure what was going on around me, but I remembered well what I was reading.)

The lesson? The experts know best for the average person, but they may not know best for you. Experiment with what works for you: time, place, environment. Then, make that the place where you routinely study.

Pace yourself

Cramming has rarely helped anyone. While you may pick up a few more pieces of information, you may not even remember them when you face the test because you are tired or because you made your brain tired by overfilling it at the last minute. Research has consistently shown that studying smaller pieces of information for a shorter amount of time on a regular basis results in better learning. Your brain and body are not stretched into exhaustion—and you have the opportunity for repetition over time, which helps get information into short-term memory and then from short-term memory into long-term memory.

Compare (associate)

Using comparisons (associations) puts your associative memory in charge, and the further you get from age 15, the stronger your associative memory becomes and the weaker your rote memory becomes. So, use your brain wisely: use associative memory.

Compare words. Is the new word like the word in your native language? If yes, what are the differences? Concentrating on these differences and finding patterns among them can speed your vocabulary acquisition tremendously. I have overseen programs in related languages (e.g., students who have learned Russian studying Serbian, students who have studied Spanish learning Portuguese, students who have studied German learning Swedish, etc.), in which learners were able to move so rapidly in the acquisition of the second language from the same language family that we cut the length of the course in half. I have personally felt this effect. In 1990, I learned enough Czech in a few hours each week to go to Prague in three months and conduct negotiations with the State Publishing House, without an interpreter present, to acquire teaching materials I needed for my program; I used a book called *Czech through Russian* (Townsend and Komar), Russian being a language I possess at a near-native level, and once I saw the patterns, I really needed less than 100 hours to get to a usable level of the Czech language. Likewise, based on my knowledge of Spanish, I was able to pick up enough Portuguese to participate in professional conversations within days of arriving in Brazil. You can do the same if you become good at noticing similarities between your language and another one you know or between new and old information.

Compare grammar between your native language and your target language or between another language you know and your target language. Where does the grammar match? Where does it not match? What patterns of comparison can you find?

Compare anything—two texts, cultural ways of doing things, people. Whatever you compare will end up in your memory through association.

Making comparisons comes more naturally to those we call levelers, a learning style that reflects a preference for finding similarities among items (seeing pears and apples, levelers will note that they have seen fruit). To sharpeners, a learning style that reflects a penchant for finding differences among items (seeing pears and apples, sharpeners will note that they have seen pears and apples).[1] If you are a natural sharpener, you can teach yourself to find similarities. Make a Venn diagram (two intersecting circles). In one circle, list what you see in the target language phenomenon you are studying (word, grammar, text, function [action], culture) that is different from your language. In the other circle, do the opposite: write what you see in your language that is different from the target language. In the middle, where the circles intersect, write you see as pretty much the same between them.[2]

---

[1] More information on levelers and sharpeners, sometimes called lumpers and splitters, can be found in works by Leaver (1997, 2019), Ehrman and Leaver (2002), and Messick (1976).

[2] If you have trouble doing this, start with something easy, like apples and oranges. Apples = red, tart, dry-ish, white meat. Oranges = orange, sweet, juicy, white rind. In the center: fruit, seeds, skin, stems. Do this a lot, and it will become instinctive.

Make connections (use mnemonics)

Similar to making comparisons is the strategy of making connections. Sound connections work, like remembering that you have to go to **s**tore, then go to the post offices because you need **s**tamps, and then pick up your child, friend, or sibling at **s**chool: s-s-s. Strings on fingers—you use those to remember what you want to buy at the grocery store, right? Well, maybe not you, but many people do. You may tell yourself you have to buy three things and focus on the concept of three, connecting the items to the three things: eggs, milk, and cheese. These are called mnemonic devices. They can be based on humor, imagery, uniqueness, alliteration (like *store, school, stamps*), key words, acronyms, and as many more little techniques as you can think of. The bottom line is that there is a strong connection that will remind you of the word, rule, or text you are trying to remember.

Sound connections in a foreign language, for example, German, can help you remember the word, *Nacht*, if you think that it sounds like *English* night. The English words *yellow blue bus* use imagery and sound connections can help you remember *ya lyublyu vas* (*I love you* in Russian)—even if you actually said, "yellow blue bus," a native speaker of Russian would understand what you are trying to say.

Mnemonic devices are limited only by your imagination. Start using them today, and in a week, you will be good at them!

Use roots[3]

Although this strategy may not work in all languages, it will work in many, if not most, languages. Different lan-

---

[3] Romanization of foreign alphabets is used in this book in order to make the concepts accessible to all readers, not just those studying a particular language.

guages form words in varying ways, so if you know how roots work in one language, you may need to learn how they work differently in another. Using roots, though, is important across the board.

Using roots can be very important in languages like Arabic, where word formation is based on roots.[4] If you know that the k-t-b combination in Arabic has a basic meaning associated with writing, it will be easier to remember words like *kitab* (book—the result of writing), *maktab* (office—the place where one writes), and *maktaba* (bookstore or library—the place where writing is sold or kept). Even *maktub* (fate, destiny) will be easier to remember if the literal translation is understood as "it is written."

Russian word formation happens differently, but it still makes use of roots. Take *rabot-*, for example, which has the basic meaning of *work*. Just knowing this gives you access to a very long list of words that you should be able to remember instantly (associative/binding memory here) even if you are hearing or seeing (or making them up) for the first time: *rabota* (job, work), *rabotnik* (worker), *rabotyaga* (workaholic), and *rabochij* [den', etc.] (working [day, etc.]). If you learn the basic meaning of prefixes and suffixes, you can expand any list even further, e.g., *govor-* (basic meaning as a root: speaking; by itself, also means dialect), *zagovor* (conspiracy), *pogovorka* (saying, proverb), *ogovorka* (misspeaking), *razgovor* (conversation), *govorit'* (to speak), *dogovor* (treaty), *govorun* (chatterbox), and the list goes on.[5]

---

4 According to Ryding, (2005) there are between 5000 and 6500 lexical roots in Arabic.

5 A good source of Russian roots, along with prefixes and suffixes, is *Roots of the Russian Language: An Elementary Guide to Word-building* (Patrick, 1989).

If you know how to use roots, you will be able to expand your vocabulary tremendously both for recognition and for making up words when you are not sure of the word, and for guessing right. You can probably find a list of roots for your language on the Internet or in a book somewhere. Check it out!

Structure your learning

Organize the material you are studying. Your brain learns better when new information is connected with old information and when information is entered into and stored in memory in clusters. Try grouping your notes into categories, keeping in mind that it is better in language learning to learn words and grammar in context. So, ensure that your notes have a context and put new words and grammar into memory in context, i.e. full sentences and texts. Some learners, especially those who are analytic,[6] linear,[7] or mechanical,[8] can remember better if they outline the texts they are studying.

---

[6] Analytic learners disassemble information into component parts, in contrast to synthetic learners who use pieces to build a composite new whole (Ehrman & Leaver, 2002; Leaver, 1997, 2019; Leaver, Ehrman, & Shekhtman, 2002).

[7] Linear learners, also called sequential learners, prefer to receive and practice new material in a step-by-step fashion, in contrast to nonlinear, or random, learners who prefer to receive material in the raw, not organized in any particular fashion, so that they can organize it in their own way (Ehrman & Leaver, 2002; Leaver, 1997, 2019; Leaver, Ehrman, & Shekhtman, 2002).

[8] Mechanical learners are a subset of motor learners, who learn through movement: full body (kinesthetic learners), touching things (haptic learners), and writing/typing (mechanical learners). They are said to have motor or mechanical memory. When they feel something they have learned, it is easy to recall, and they enter information into memory through feeling it via large (body) or small (hand) muscles (Leaver, 1997).

Think Yourself into Becoming a Language Learning Super Star!

Elaborate and rehearse

Before you can recall information, you have to get it to your long-term memory. Repetition will get it into your short-term memory (we are talking about seconds here not hours and days), but it has to move out of short-term memory into long-term memory, a matter of encoding the information visually, acoustically, or semantically if you want to be able to be able to make use of it later.

You could continue to repeat and repeat along the lines of the Russian saying, "povtorenie mat' ucheniya" (repetition is the mother of learning). Very likely you have done a lot of that. This would be called maintenance rehearsal, and it really does work at maintaining the information in short-term memory and, with enough rehearsal, in long-term memory. Maintenance rehearsal is most suitable for songs and poems—long lines of fixed texts—but elaborative rehearsal works better for learning a language.

Elaborative rehearsal is a matter of, as the term says, elaborating on the new information. Make all those connections mentioned earlier, but also find other ways to use the information and use all your senses in doing so: write it, read it, speak it, listen to it—in a number of different environments. Then, move on to use the information (words, grammar, functions, cultural information) in new and unique contexts. Talk to yourself (yes, seriously, if you have no other partner, you still have yourself). Find opportunities to use it with peers, in class, and outside class with native speakers. Write a short story or article using what you are studying. Don't just look at or read a new vocabulary word; look for it in an article online—figure out how many different ways it can be used and in what contexts, and how those contexts differ. Then, use the word in a conversation, in writing a journal note, or in any other writing or speaking application that seems appropriate.

The more you involve yourself in elaborative rehearsal through different kinds of activities, the deeper the level of processing will be, and more effective encoding into long-term will result (Craik & Lockhart, 1972). The bottom line with elaborative rehearsal is to not just do one thing with the new information. Try doing something with the new information or words three different times on three different days. (Why three applications work to enhance memory, I don't know, and I doubt any one scientist would say—or support—three as a magic number. Nonetheless, it does work for me and has worked for many of my students. Three uses over three days and that word is mine, or theirs, nearly forever. Try it, and see if three is a magic number for you, too.)

Visualize concepts

Visualizing what you are reading or hearing in your language can help you to remember it. Look at the photographs, charts, and other graphics in your textbooks or the authentic materials you are working with. Where there are no illustrations, you could create your own. If you do, make them colorful!

working strategically = less stress and more learning

Develop your memory muscle by using it every chance you get!

Time Off
Marinating the Mind

Acquisition of a language does not occur in one setting, one course, or one year. It goes without saying, then, that language study will not be continuous, at least in the sense of every day without break. Of course, there will be breaks. Though many students, especially those in intensive courses, worry that they will lose some of what they have gained while they are away from their studies, that is usually not the case.

You see, language proficiency progress comes from both conscious learning and unconscious learning—and something I call the marination factor, which is related to the unconscious factor. As with cooking, "marination" requires taking some time out and walking away from active work. Just as meat does not remain the same while marinating, neither does your brain. It is busy sorting and categorizing the information you have been stuffing into it during you active conscious learning days. Now, the brain has time to stop receiving new information but does not rest because it is busy making better sense and organization of what it has already received. *This time is essential for good learning.*

So, what can and should you do while you are physically away from your studies? The sections that follow contain suggestions that I have found to work for my students.

Account for the marination factor

Give your conscious mind a rest and let your subconscious organize the grammar and vocabulary you have learned. While up until now, you may have felt strong conscious control over how you used your language skills—your choices in vocabulary and phraseology—once you let go and give your unconscious brain some space and free rein, you may be surprised at what happens. At first, you may think you have lost proficiency. That is likely not true. Rather, once items have marinated, you will find yourself using expressions *automatically*, without conscious effort. *That* is what we call language *acquisition* (as opposed to language *learning*, which is conscious speaking and conscious study).

Conduct an individualized review

Here is a chance to spend time on what you think you need to review, not what a teacher has assigned you to review. Self-assess. Do you have identifiable gaps? Go for it. Fill them in. If you feel like it, spend *some* time regularly reviewing but not every day and not copious amounts of time. This is time for your body and your conscious brain to rest. Go play, and let your unconscious brain do its job.

Do some leisure listening and reading

If you really feel pressed to keep on working on your language, then find a book or a movie in your language. Read or listen for pleasure, and be pleased with what you understand automatically. Don't worry about what you don't understand. Read or watch again—and again if it matters to you that you may have missed some important information in the book or movie. Alternatively, be pleased with what you *can* understand, and let it go at that. This is your time off!

Try out your language skills

If you have a chance to spend time with native speakers, do it. Conversations on casual topics will improve your language proficiency in general. If you are at a more advanced level, pick up a short translation job. It will be a fun stretch and bring you some money, too.

Think Yourself into Becoming a Language Learning Super Star!

rest + minimum language use = relaxed and re-invigorated move forward

Let the marination factor work for you!

Betty Lou Leaver Ph.D.

Remembering, Forgetting, and Lapses

Just to reinforce the matter—or in case you are skipping around in this book and did not see the earlier memory discussion; there are three stages to memory: awareness/attention, encoding/storing, and recall/retrieval. In this section, we are focused on what happens after you have learned something and need to use it.

When you want to remember, you will need to recall the information you have learned. One of three things can happen, and we have all experienced all three: we remember it perfectly (yippee—hope that happens always, but it does not), we remember it imperfectly (oh, too typical), or do not remember it all (even if we remember having spent time studying it). Knowing what has happened in each case brings us to a point of orienting our study and actions for better recall as well as teaching us not to beat ourselves up when we have a glitch or lapse.

Remembering perfectly

For perfect recall to happen, you have to be aware of what you are learning, let's say it is the word, *magazin*, in Russian, a false cognate that means *store*. You must be aware that the word means *store* in English, and it would help to have an image of a Russian-style store in your mind.

You then store the word, together with its picture if you have one, in your long-term memory through repetition and elaborate rehearsal. Perhaps you see a Russian store in some news reports (written or broadcast). Perhaps you use it in a role play in class. Perhaps you write a little story about how you would stock a store. The ways to store this word are limitless, but elaborate rehearsal works better than simple repetition.

Now you need to use the word for a discussion or conversation. Or, perhaps you are given a picture of a store on a quiz and have to identify the picture, using the Russian word *magazin*. To do that, you have to recall the word—and you do.

Remembering imperfectly

You may well have noticed all the important aspects of the word and stored it solidly, but when you are asked to recall it, you identify the word as meaning *magazine*. Tricked by the false cognate! But you know better! You paid special attention to the fact that it is a false cognate. What happened?

You have experienced retrieval error. Something went wrong. We don't know what it is—and it probably won't happen the next time. Still, it happened this time, and that caused you embarrassment or a lower grade. In retrieval error, you have trouble pulling together all the parts associated with a piece of information. Colors, shapes, intensity, semantics, image, etc. are stored in different "compartments," and your working memory has to open all those compartments and pull the piece of information back together properly for perfect recall to occur. It is amazing that most of the time we do have perfect recall.

In this case, a connection should exist in your mind between the word that sounds like *magazine* (meaning *store* in Russian and *journal* in English) and two pictures: store and journal. The retrieval error that occurred was hearing the Russian word and connecting it with the English picture. It happens. Brush it off, and go on. We cannot prevent retrieval error. It just happens. Just like in your native language when you get your "mords wixed" or pull up the wrong image. We have all experienced retrieval error and more than once. I once "retrieved" the word *bardak* (*brothel*) in Russian when I was really searching for *baidarka* (*canoe/kayak*). I very much confused the person I was with, who did not speak English, so it took a little effort to unwind what had happened. So, again, brush it off, and go on.

Not remembering

Forgetting can happen when you start with incomplete understanding without realizing it, encode something improperly, or have some form of memory impairment. And then sometimes, everything was understood and properly encoded—and right on the tip of your tongue but does not roll off. That happens not just in your foreign language; that happens also in your native language.

Incomplete understanding.

If you only partially understand, there will be little to remember because you will not have all the parts of the information needed for encoding properly. So, only pieces are going to make the trip to your long-term memory, making it not possible to retrieve the whole of the information. So, don't leave a class or a study session until you fully, completely, no-questions-asked understand.

If you indeed do not have information stored to make a perfect recall, time to spend more time with the information, whether it is words, phrases, texts, grammar points, or cultural tidbits. Read, read, read. Reading provides for elaborate rehearsal. If you know something in part, it allows you to complete the full picture. If you know something weakly, all the extra repetition will have you know it strongly, which is what you need for perfect recall.

Improper encoding

Similar to incomplete understanding, if you misunderstand something, you will "encode" it (store it) inaccurately, which may make it impossible to retrieve. Paying careful attention helps. Make sure when you repeat it, you repeat it correctly

For listening and speaking, think about building your ear-sharpening skills. A lot of sounds in your target language do not sound like they do in English; there may be a similar sound (or not), and there is a pretty big range of "coming close" (as in the aforementioned *yellow blue bus* for *ya lyublyu vas*) that permits a native speaker to understand you though you are speaking with a very strong accent. The other way around, however, does not work well. If you cannot say it right, chances are you are not hearing it right in a classroom environment where the teacher and other learners can help. When you are watching movies or listening to broadcasts alone, you may not understand a word that you really do know because you have been mispronouncing it or pronouncing it poorly. Go back, ask your teacher or native-speaker friend for help, and get it right! If it is properly encoded, you will remember it when you need to (except for an occasional, unpredictable, pesky, and fortunately rare retrieval error.

An important condition in learning that can affect coding is situated cognition (Brown, Collins, & Duguid, 1989). Situated cognition research tells us that our acquisition of knowledge is constructed within and linked to the activity, context, and/or culture in which it was learned.

Memory impairment

Certain medicines, such as antihistamines and allergy meds, as discussed earlier in the section on chemicals can block memory and make you seem to forget. You can compensate by increasing the number of memory strategies you use.

There are other things that can impair memory, too, like alcohol and drugs; if you want to be a super star language learner, avoid them.

learning = you control your brain
forgetting = your brain controls you

Accept an imperfect memory (life is imperfect), and work to improve everything that you do control!

Betty Lou Leaver Ph.D.

Cognition:
Wrong Thinking That Impedes Your Learning Progress;
Right Thinking That Speeds Up Your Progress

Betty Lou Leaver Ph.D.

All too often learners are held back from complete success by obstacles of their own making through just plain wrong thinking. We call these kinds of wrong thinking cognitive distortions. They creep into our thinking rather naturally, but we need to fight them off because when we let cognitive distortions creep into our thinking, we end up interpreting events in such a way that fuels emotions such as anxiety, depression, or anger—and that puts up barriers to language learning success.

As noted in the Acknowledgements, if you read that section, Dr. Funke, colleague of mine at the DLIFLC suggested a list of cognitive distortions that have a particularly strong influence (read that: impedance) in learning a foreign language.[9] Although researchers have identified dozens of cognitive distortions, many of them are generic. As such, they do have some impact on language learning. For the sake of space, in this book, I am including in the sections that follow those cognitive distortions that I have found to be especially pertinent for language learners. If you are interested, you can Google the term, *cognitive distortion*, and find quite a long list of cognitive distortions that researchers have found.

---

[9] Unfortunately, Dr. Funke never published any of his work. What I have of his lists comes from handouts and our joint work with learners and faculty.

Betty Lou Leaver Ph.D.

All-or-Nothing Thinking

In this kind of thinking, there is no shade of gray. There is not even black-and-white. Rather, everything is perceived as an extreme. Good or bad. Right or wrong. Success or failure. In all-or-nothing thinking, there is no middle ground though we all know that life is general is mostly middle ground.

Defining all-or-nothing thinking

All-or-nothing thinking says that if something happens once, it will always happen. It can be a result of perfectionism and can lead to the unwillingness or inability to take risks. This is not helpful since learning a language requires taking frequent risks—making a guess at a word, saying something that you do not really know how to say but trying to come close, and more.

On a broader level, if you are struggling in a language course (almost everyone does at one time or another), you mistakenly assume that you do not have the talent to manage the course or to learn the language. That in turn may result in your becoming depressed and not wanting to try anything new; you only want to do your assignments and hope you won't be too embarrassed by any mistakes. In all-or-nothing thinking, you erroneously conclude that if you cannot do your regular assignments well, then you certainly would not be able to go beyond what has been assigned. Risk-taking, which is essential to language learning success, is out of the question.

Here are some ways in which learners exhibit all-or-nothing thinking:

- When you do not receive 100% on a test, you tell yourself you are failing and will not be able to pass any future tests;

- When you make mistakes with a couple of expressions in an important conversation with a native speaker or as part of a role play, you feel depressed all evening;
- When others in the class seem to do better at a role-play than you, you know that you do not have the same level of talent as your classmates, and you despair; and
- When you cannot understand all the words in a reading assignment, broadcast, or movie, you know the language is beyond your abilities, and you give up, not crediting yourself for all the words you *did* understand.

all-or-nothing thinking = nothing gained linguistically or emotionally

Avoiding all-or-nothing thinking

The first step toward avoiding anything successfully is to recognize it. Are you often or occasionally exhibiting all-or-nothing thinking? What prompts it? When did it start? Was there a single event or a bad week?

Use metacognitive strategies[10] to take control of any situation in which you find yourself exhibiting all-or-nothing thinking. Rather than letting feelings dominate your reaction to imperfections in your performance, keep track of how you are really doing, recording how much you have learned and what you can do in the language. You will see

---

10 Metacognitive (means "above thinking") strategies relate to thinking about thinking, like planning your study, monitoring your progress, and rewarding yourself for success.

that your dire predictions about not being able to learn the language are not true.

Here are some metacognitive strategies that can be useful in avoiding all-or-nothing thinking:

- Review your performance daily or weekly and self-assess your performance;
- Analyze your self-assessment as to whether it is objective or reflects all-or-nothing thinking; and
- If you find you have *some* problems in learning your language, identify them, determine what you need to do to overcome them (your teacher may be able to help you with this), and then do it.

avoidance = action

Take charge of your cognition by turning to metacognition!

Betty Lou Leaver Ph.D.

Overgeneralization

Overgeneralization is somewhat related to all-or-nothing thinking. However, it is not marked by swinging between extremes (either *all* is fine or *nothing* is fine), but in overgeneralization, you assume that one small thing is typical of everything or apply the characteristics of one event to all events.

Defining overgeneralization

Overgeneralization occurs when you single out one negative event as a never-ending pattern of defeat. Doing this often prevents you from moving on or seeing things as they really are. Overgeneralization often results in depression or anxiety.

You can also make linguistic overgeneralizations. Seeing an emerging pattern in some grammatical phenomena or in word formation, you assume this pattern applies to all circumstances, but it does not. This is not a cognitive distortion; it is good thinking and probably how you learned your first language. Unlike cognitive distortions, which are unhelpful, linguistic generalizations are helpful and overgeneralizations will, at worst, land you in a situation where your language is wrong (but often understood), as in saying the equivalent of *foots*, instead of *feet*, or pluralizing *a deer* as *some deers* instead of *some deer*.

Here are some ways in which learners exhibit overgeneralization that is indeed a cognitive distortion:

- Your teacher points out some errors you have made on a homework assignment, and you assume that you do not understanding anything about the assignment although most of your answers were correct;
- One of your classmates makes a joke about you (re-

ally, the classmate did not mean to be offensive and thought that you would laugh at yourself), and you assume that your classmate does not like you—or that all your classmates do not like you; or

- You meet someone from the native culture with whom you do not click and assume that all native speakers are like the one you just met.

generalization = learning aid
overgeneralization = learning impediment

Avoiding overgeneralization

As stated with the previous cognitive distortion, the first step toward avoiding anything successfully is to recognize it. Are you often or occasionally overgeneralizing? What prompts it? Finding the prompt for overgeneralization can help turn it off.

With overgeneralizations, you can get help. First, start with yourself. Ask yourself, am I overgeneralizing? Then explore whether your assumption is true. Don't stop there. Move beyond yourself and ask your teacher for clarification if you think you are overgeneralizing; the teacher can also confirm whether or not you are overgeneralizing.

finding the prompt for overgeneralization = turning off the prompt for overgeneralization

Check your assumptions for truth!

Mental Filtering

Although we might think that filtering out bad thoughts and experiences could contribute to a happier experience in life, mental filtering is generally considered negative. It is a cognitive distortion that filters out the positive and retains the negative. That often leads to depression and anxiety. So, mental filtering is not something to be embraced.

Defining mental filtering

Life has good, bad, and neutral moments. However, learners who are trapped by the cognitive distortion of mental filtering see only the bad moments. Whatever is neutral or good gets interpreted as bad. In this kind of thinking, you cannot march past or squeeze past the "filter" or obstacle that you have unconsciously placed in front of yourself. By focusing exclusively on negatives, your view of reality becomes distorted.

Here are some examples of mental filtering:

- Your teacher corrects your pronunciation—even though your pronunciation in general is good (you actually know that, and your teacher has told you that, after the correction, you find yourself tongue-tied, focusing on how "bad" your pronunciation is and reluctant to speak in front of others because you are not embarrassed by your pronunciation;
- On a test, you make a mistake with correct usage of one class of verbs, and after that you start making mistakes on other classes as well, growing increasingly certain that you cannot understand how verbs are conjugated when really you had a good handle on them until this particular test; and/or
- Two of your classmates who are working on a project

with you tell you they really like how you organized the Internet research results that all three of you have gathered and, noticing that they both gathered more, you assume that the compliment about your organization was really a way of telling you that you had not done your fair share of research.

looking for the negative = finding the negative

Avoiding mental filtering

Once again, the clear way to avoid mental filtering, or any cognitive distortion, is to move beyond cognition to metacognition. In this case, you need to prove to yourself that there are many positive aspects of your learning progress—and to *know* that because *feeling* it will not come until after you remove the filter.

Here are some ways to use metacognition to help you eliminate the filter:

- Keep a journal for a week, and every time something positive happens, write it down—this requires you to focus on the positive, not the negative.

- Read your journal at the end of the week, note down the number of positive events, and allow yourself to realize that perhaps you are in a mostly good situation.

- Especially if you are having trouble staying focused on the positive to capture all the good moments, ask a friend in the class to help you (perhaps you can even both keep journals and note down your own positive moments as well as the positive moments you have noticed for each); it never hurts to have someone who can help you with putting a positive

spin on things.
- Find the incurably optimistic learners among your classmates and start palling around with them.

looking for the positive = finding the positive

Look for the positive—always!

Betty Lou Leaver Ph.D.

Mustification

I love the word *mustification*. You will not find it in any dictionary. Dr. Funke coined it, based on the word *must*, to indicate the unreasonable expectations we set for ourselves. Too many expectations, and we cannot move; we have tied ourselves up on our own with our own requirements not necessarily having anything to do with what is externally expected of us.

Mustification ends up adding too many tasks to be handled well and on time. This creates a sense of guilt.

Defining mustification

Mustification focuses on the internal state, not external requirements. It happens when we use words like *would, should, ought,* and *must* about ourselves. In essence, mustification encourages whipping oneself with these words and then feeling guilt or self-pity because you don't or can't do these things!

Here are some ways to know when you are under the spell of mustification:

- You find yourself saying things like "I should have done that differently" or "I have to do this" associated with guilt feelings;

- Knowing that reading a lot improves proficiency so you plan on reading 5-10 pages of authentic articles every night—and when you don't succeed in doing that, you feel guilty and mad at yourself; and/or

- You spent too much time on grammar and did not have time to review vocabulary for your test, and you tell yourself: I should have studied more

Avoiding mustification

Hey, take it easy on yourself? If you fall asleep while studying, don't feel guilty. Understand that your body needs rest and is taking over for your brain, which is not allowing it. You need sleep to perform well.

Realize that all the "musts" in the world really come from you. Yes, you have deadlines and projects that have been assigned, but you chose to take the course, right? Or, if the course is part of a career pattern or job, you chose that career pattern or job, right? All those other musts are coming from within you.

That does not mean taking it easy in class or blowing off assignments but rather being aware of the reality in which you live. Prepare to meet the deadlines coming your way (that will turn into musts if you do not prepare for them) by setting up a schedule with what you can reasonably complete each day—and then do it. If, instead of that or even in spite of that, you did not do a good job of time management for test preparation or project turn-in this time, learn from it and do better next time.

strong self-compassion = strong ultimate performance

You have enough "musts" in your life; do not arbitrarily add more!

Personalization

Language students and teachers use the term personalization to mean taking something new being taught in the foreign language and adapting the information to your own circumstances so that you can use the information (text, phrases) whenever you need it in your personal life. For example, you might be listening to a clip that shows two people ordering something from a restaurant. Then, you re-enact the scene with your classmates, but you make your own choices, not the choices from the clip: the food you want to eat, how you address the wait staff, how you discuss the menu with your eating partner, and which of the various expressions used to order you will take for your own use ("I would like," "how about," "could I get," "would you please bring me," etc.—you probably never noticed that there are some many correct ways to order. This is not a cognitive distortion. This is a helpful and needed form of personalization.

When we talk about personalization as a cognitive distortion, we are talking about something very different. It is about making everything about you, and it is a negative way of going about learning. Every mistake is your fault. Every culturally inappropriate expression is your fault. Did you get a bad test score? Your fault. (Test results, really, are an ascertaining of two things: how well a teacher has taught and how well a student has learned.) Didn't get your homework in on time because you got sick? You are a bad person. This type of personalization is debilitating; it erects barriers in your learning path.

Defining personalization

Personalization, simply put, is seeing yourself as responsible for events that you cannot control. It involves expecting too much from yourself because you think you should be able to control everything in your life; when you can't, you blame yourself. One reason personalization presents as distorted is because it is so over the top: often, the things you personalize you could not possibly control or be responsible for.

Here are some examples of what learners who personalize say:

- "Even though I was sick, I should have completed all my work;"
- "I should get my classmates to be less unruly because it is really interfering with instruction in the class and disconcerts the teacher;" and/or
- "My group did not do well on our project; I should have put more time into it."

I am responsible for myself, everyone else, and everything = not true, not possible

Avoiding personalization

Personalization is a deviously difficult cognitive distortion to overcome. It is easy to say, "it's not about you." (It really isn't about you, you know.) It's easy to tell you what not to do: don't blame yourself for the general state of things that you have no control over. (You did not create that state, right?) Negative advice is equally easy: don't think you should have done something more, longer, or better—and because you did not, you are a bad person. (You do really know that you are a good person, right?) What you did is what you did. What happened is what happened. Don't blame yourself; don't blame others.

Don't is easy to say but hard to do. How do you verify that the absence of something is actually occurring? Obviously, that is difficult, but not impossible. But why go there? Why try to avoid a tendency to personalize the hard way. Instead, look at what you can *do*—and then do it.

Here are some examples of what you can do:

- look for things you can control: good study habits and doing your best;
- on a regular basis, make a list of all the things you have done well that day or week, including non-language activities (and definitely non-testing activities)—perhaps what you did to help someone in your class or in the community (that counts a lot) or your involvement with a special cause (if you are going to personalize something, personalize how good you are);
- when you feel like something is your fault, make a 2-column list and write in the left column the things that you have no control over or that are the fault of something or someone other than yourself and in the right column the things that truly are your fault (likely, there will be none or just a few—and if there are some, make a plan to fix them); and/or
- find and do things at least every other day that you do well and that make you feel good about yourself.

spreading out among others what you would otherwise personalize = more accurate view of reality

Life is personal, almost always, but try to find objectivity within it!

Betty Lou Leaver Ph.D.

Jumping to Conclusions

I think we all know what jumping to conclusions means—drawing conclusions that are no based on an adequate amount of input. Almost always, these conclusions are negative in nature. (There is also the situation in which someone jumps to an unwarranted positive conclusion—I really am going to win the lottery because our store won the last two months. This is delusion or extreme optimism, but it is not a cognitive distortion.)

Defining jumping to conclusions

As a cognitive distortion, jumping to conclusions occurs when you reach a conclusion without having all the facts. When you do this, the conclusion is unwarranted. This happens when you don't distinguish between what you have observed and what you have inferred or assumed. Psychologists call this the "inference observation confusion."

Jumping to conclusions is, really, mind reading and forecasting the future and is usually quite inaccurate. It frequently happens when you take one or two facts and build a picture with them that may very likely be unreal. Here are some examples:

- you did poorly on a test even though you studied for it (you just had a bad day) and now you are scared and certain that you are going to fail the course;
- you are having trouble remembering idioms that your teacher has assigned you (for the first time), and you assume that is because you are just not someone who can learn idioms; and/or
- your teacher made what sounded like a negative comment about you (the teacher did not; you mis-

heard), and now you avoid the teacher's eyes because you know the teacher thinks poorly of you.

jumping to conclusions = unnecessarily jumping into an abyss

Avoiding jumping to conclusions

When you are sure that things are going really, really poorly, take a deeper look. Very likely, you are jumping to conclusions. Things don't typically go really, really poorly in language classes, and, of all teachers, most language teachers want their students to succeed and are open to helping them. About those idioms, give yourself time to learn them. Time helps with many things.

Below are some specific things you can do to help yourself.

- When you have reached a conclusion, check your conclusion against facts, lining up whatever objective information you can find;
- Ask someone—a teacher or a peer—if your conclusion is justified, as in
  - if you think you have no aptitude for language, ask your teacher (or take an aptitude test);
  - if you think you are coming across as unprepared or incompetent, ask your teacher;
  - if you think your teacher does not like you, ask your peers; and/or
  - if you don't think you are the greatest thing since sliced bread, ask your mother!
- Write down all the conclusions you have made about

yourself and your course and undertake some research (documents, peers, teachers) to see how many of them are justified (probably not many).

patience + facts + research = justified conclusions

Look before you leap!

Betty Lou Leaver Ph.D.

The Brainscape in Language Learning

Betty Lou Leaver Ph.D.

There are some psychological phenomena that exist that are not exactly cognitive distortions but have a similar effect on learning capacity and performance. They might be called cognitive distractions, except that they also have a strong emotional component.

Three representative "cognitive distractions" include tolerance of ambiguity, ego boundaries, and mental management. The uniqueness of this trio is that they are continua with strong poles and weak poles. The strong poles are the ability to tolerate ambiguity, thin ego boundaries that allow you to approach the native speaker with comfort, and mental management that puts you in charge of your own performance. The weak poles are inability to tolerate ambiguity, thick ego boundaries that put barriers between you and native speakers, and lack of mental management,

Betty Lou Leaver Ph.D.

Tolerance of Ambiguity

Do you feel lost if you cannot understand 100% of everything going on around you in your classroom, including every single word you hear? Do you need to know every work in a reading text, broadcast, or movie before you can understand what you are reading or listening to? If you answered yes to these questions, then you have a low tolerance of ambiguity.

We meet ambiguity in many places in life. Anywhere we find things less than black-and-white, we meet ambiguity. Gray areas intrigue some people; they have high tolerance of ambiguity. Gray areas trouble other people; they have low tolerance of ambiguity. For some people, ambiguity is even perceived as an existential threat (Budner, 1962).

Unfortunately for language learners, languages are high in ambiguity, especially if you are looking for direct correspondences with your native language and culture. There is no way around it: if you want to become a good language learner, you will need to work on developing a level of comfort in dealing with ambiguity.

Defining tolerance of ambiguity

Ambiguity occurs when clarity is lacking in what you have heard or read. It could mean one thing; it could mean another; or, you cannot get enough of the thought to understand anything at all.

It is important to realize that language (not just foreign language), by its very nature, is ambiguous. People are different one from another; their thoughts differ; and the way in which people express their thoughts differ. So, there is always room for misunderstanding—even in your native language. In a foreign language classroom, the problem is compounded; a great amount of contradictory information is encountered in learning a foreign language, but it must be managed to be a successful learner (Brown, 2007).

If you feel uncomfortable in any of the situations below, chances are you have a low tolerance of ambiguity and will need to work to improve if you want to succeed in your language class.

- Words have multiple meanings; context decides, as in *mumkin* in Arabic which can mean *perhaps, maybe, yes,* or *no.* (Welcome to the Arabic highly contextualized way of speaking!).

- You feel lost entering a subway system in the country of the language you are studying; it does not look at all like the subway system at home.

- You are pulled into a game with native speakers and have no idea how to play it; it is not like anything you have played before.

never done, never seen, queasy stomach,
shaky hands = low tolerance of ambiguity

never done, never seen,
sheer excitement = high tolerance of ambiguity

Tolerating (managing) ambiguity

Most of the ambiguity you will probably encounter in the classroom relates to reading texts that seem unclear or not understanding some cultural differences you see in a film. However, if you are participating in a study abroad experience, changes are you will meet ambiguity many times a day. The more the culture differs from yours, the higher the amount of ambiguity. I have lived and worked in 24 countries, and even though I had learned my way around Europe, Latin America, and the Soviet Union, I still was not completely prepared for Asia or the Middle East—or, for that matter, Russia once the USSR fell.

In addition to acquiring good cognitive language learning strategies for when you encounter ambiguity in reading or listening (see Oxford, 2017). Listed below are some ways to improve your tolerance of ambiguity:

- Accept ambiguity as part of communication in any language, realizing that expecting to understand everything in another language is unrealistic (even in your native language, you do not always understand everything).
- Look for what you *can* understand and ignore what you cannot.
- Use means other than language to figure out what you do not understand: context, body language—and, when you cannot express yourself with adequate language point, gesture, body language, and other non-linguistic cues.
- Let your brain, which is an extraordinary organ, do the work of unconsciously putting meaning to the stream of words coming at you; though you may not be fully aware of it, your brain is processing incoming information, categorizing it, and organizing it.

acceptance of ambiguity = control over ambiguity

Don't panic in ambiguous environments. Find and focus on the familiar while accepting the unfamiliar!

Betty Lou Leaver Ph.D.

Ego Boundaries

Ego boundaries, also called boundaries of the mind (Hartmann, 1991), refer to someone's willingness to let someone into his or her inner circle and reflect the ego's function of distinguishing between self and non-self (i.e. someone else). When that someone else comes from another culture, the ego boundaries of a language learner (or anyone) between self and the "other" can be either thick or thin. Thick boundaries make it difficult for an individual to assimilate into another culture. Thin (permeable) boundaries make assimilation much easier. These differences are also called strong and weak ego boundaries.

Defining ego boundaries

Every learner has a barrier between "self" and "other." This is normal; this is healthy. When the boundaries are very thick, however, they do not allow the learner to build a relationship with a native speaker from the culture of the language being studied. The barrier between them is too thick, too strong. Thin boundaries are generally viewed as more favorable for developing the kinds of foreign relationships needed for the development of good intercultural understanding.

Listed below are some examples of ego boundaries:

- You do not like the taste of nearly any food in the foreign country or in your home country made by immigrants from the country whose language you are speaking;
- You do not like being touched by a native speaker, even casually, and you certainly could not walk arm-in-arm with someone of your gender though that is the custom in the country you are studying.

- If you are in a study abroad program, you look forward to the diurnal ending of the daily required activities that require mixing in with native speakers.

ego boundary = barrier between self and other

Managing thick ego boundaries

Managing or overcoming thick ego boundaries, or, using another image, thinning your boundary, can be accomplished by anyone. Those with thin boundaries need no further thinning but to just leave the minimal barriers in place for safety. Too-thin boundaries blur the distinction between self and "other," which is not good. Most activities associated with managing ego boundaries require interacting some way with the target population or culture.

Below are some ways to develop thinner boundaries.

- Spend a lot of time in-country and become actively involved with native speakers there; since familiarity reduces fear, over time, you will find yourself comfortable with your foreign counterparts.
- Develop a personal friendship with someone from the culture you are studying; it will improve your language skills and thin your ego boundaries.

familiarity = comfort level

Tear down ego walls between you and your foreign counterpart for more natural language learning success!

Mental Management

What is a goal without a plan? A dream?

Mental management techniques work at turning dreams into reality by requiring the setting of goals and establishing a clear and comprehensive (and do-able) plan. In his book, *With Winning in Mind* (2011, The Mentashowinl Management System), Lanny Bassham discusses the importance of setting goals and tracking progress. The right—and positive—mental attitude can definitely assist a person in accomplishing his or her goals.

Defining mental management

Mental management is the process of being able to improve your progress or show your prowess while under stress. Have you ever been under stress in a language course? Of course, you have!

If any of these following circumstances apply, you could benefit from training in mental management.

- You draw a blank on a test even though you know the material well.
- You have trouble sleeping the night before a big exam.
- You are so nervous during class that you cannot learn new things because you are afraid that the teacher is going to call on you at any minute.
- You have much trouble remembering the content of your assignments because you are spending time worrying about what the results of your work on your assignments will be.
- You feel nauseous during class because you are having trouble keeping up with your classmates; and/or

- you forget what you had planned to say during an in-class oral presentation on a project you have worked on for several weeks in spite of having rehearsed it six times.

stress during performance = need for mental management

Developing good mental management

If any of the conditions above describe you, time to develop some good mental management. Good mental management will get you though many difficult activities and help you improve your language performance.

Listed below are some ways to develop good mental management.

- Control your conscious thought: don't be distracted, focus on your goal, visualize you using your language well at an important event (this has the additional value of improving your self-image)—if you can visualize it, you can become it.
- Plan how you will achieve each step of your goal and visualize those steps.
- Monitor your level of stress, keeping in mind that moderate amounts of stress release adrenaline which can actually improve performance by focusing your attention and giving you better endurance.

planning + monitoring + visualization = control

Take charge of your thoughts!

Affective Dissonance:
Taming Emotions
That Get in the Way of Learning
and
Promoting Emotions That Help

Betty Lou Leaver Ph.D.

Affective dissonances parallel cognitive distortions. Just as cognitive distortions create chaos in your studying because of wrong thinking, affective dissonance can tear down your confidence in language learning so that your performance becomes less than it could possibly be because of wrong feeling.

Affective dissonance refers to when you respond emotionally and either incorrectly or inappropriately to language learning situations. Maybe you are using reasoning that is emotional in nature. Maybe you are talking to yourself in negative ways. Perhaps you are not giving yourself enough credit, mislabeling yourself, or feeling high levels of anxiety. You *can* train yourself to put aside debilitating emotions.

Betty Lou Leaver Ph.D.

Emotional Reasoning

If you are an emotional reasoner, you may get completely derailed on your journey to good language proficiency because you let your emotions rule your reason. Emotional reasoning, often lumped in with cognitive distortions (Beck, 1979), lets your emotional state, which can be a result of your academic experiences or a result of the events in your life or both, color your attitude, whether that is toward your course, your studying, your homework, your teacher, your textbook, your assignments, your classmates, or any other aspect of your academic life.

Definition of emotional reasoning

Emotional reasoning feels like you are riding a roller coaster. Your performance chugs upward, then speeds downward, over and over. Under these conditions, your performance is tracking with these emotional peaks and valleys, ups and downs, and not with your study.

Here are some examples:

- you have fallen in love, and now you and your significant other are planning a wedding, taking massive amounts of time away from your studies; you reason that you need to spend time on your love, not your language literacy, because love is enduring and perhaps language isn't (wow, one could easily argue the opposite);

- you owe a lot of debts, and now one of your creditors is after you to pay up or else; while scrambling to pay your debt, you may actually take on another job (not a good idea when your studies are already an important job), and you are tired in class; and/or

- you have fallen sick enough that your doctor wants

you to rest up for a few days, but you do not want to miss class; you are experiencing anxiety.

*emotional reasoning = making decisions
based on feelings, not thinking*

Eliminating emotion from reasoning

You clearly cannot remove all emotions or opportunities for deep emotional experiences in your life, nor would you want to. What you need to do is not allow emotion to take over your decision-making. There are techniques for doing that.

Here are some ways to eliminate the emotion from reasoning:

- separate outside distractive emotions from your classroom experience; make a commitment to yourself to focus on home matters at home, social matters when you are in society, and academic matters at school—and not mix and match;
- when you feel anxious, take a step back, identify the source, and answer the question as to whether the anxiety is warranted (you may not be able to do this alone though many learners can; if it seems important and you cannot take a step back, seek professional health, which will be worth it; and
- recognize the tug-of-war between your thoughts and your feelings, and, if you can, give the upper hand to thoughts.

identify source = lower anxiety

Reasoning is a cognitive function; keep it that way!

Self-Guidance

Self-guidance, self-talk, self-regulation is communication with ourselves and has been observed even in young children (Vygotsky, 1978). Self-guidance can be used to shore ourselves up or tear ourselves down and is a form of affective dissonance.

In language learning, self-guidance can be positive and promote our soaring to success. Or, it can be negative and push us into flailing into failure. Once recognized, the proper kind of self-guidance can replace debilitating self-guidance.

Defining self-guidance

Self-guidance that is disabling uses such cognitive distortions as filtering and personalizing—to the point of catastrophizing. Negative self-guidance is a powerful tool of self-destruction: motivation, self-esteem, and self-confidence all tumble. (Positive self-talk, on the other hand, brings up significant increases in motivation, self-esteem, and self-confidence.)

Below are statements made by real-life learners who were unconsciously ascribe to negative self-guidance.

- "I try, but I just can't do it."
- "I'll never learn all this vocabulary."
- "I just don't get grammar."
- "I'm not talented at language learning."

negative self-talk = self-fulfilling prophecy

Talking yourself into success

In contrast to negative self-talk, positive self-talk can promote success. Say positive things often enough, and you will believe them.

Below are some of the kinds of things you can say.

- I can do it; I've done harder things.
- I can learn this vocabulary if I use the memorization techniques I was taught.
- My friend loves grammar; I bet s/he will help me; if s/he gets it, I can, too.
- I don't have to be talented; I just have to be diligent and use good learning strategies.

Say "you are a good language learning" repetitively = you believe you are a good language learner

Think *can*, not cannot!

Disqualifying the Positive

Disqualifying the positive says a lot about your own self-esteem. It is a case where you are always putting yourself down, and this probably happens in other areas as well, not just in language learning. When you do not understand how marvelous you are (even if you are not the top student in the classroom—there are so many other ways to be a good language learner and a good person than a high test score), you start looking for what is wrong with you. When you do that, you start seeing your negative qualities (c'mon, we all have them, and if we look hard enough, we will see them, and if we are honest enough, we will admit them) and overlooking all your positive qualities, either personal or related to study and performance even when the positive qualities outnumber the negative qualities. When you do *that*, it becomes difficult to be a good learner.

Defining how learners disqualify the positive

Disqualifying the positive happens when you say to yourself that your successes do not really count because this is just the easy stuff; you will not do well on the hard stuff. It happens when you focus on a negative aspect of something you do or even your perception of who you are. It happens when you fear the future because you know the future will reveal your incompetence no matter how well you have done up until now.

Do you think any of these things that indicate that you are disqualifying the positive?

- My teacher thinks I'm great, but she does not really know me; I know so much more about myself, and it is not really all that good so I hope she does not find out.

- I have good relationships with my classmates, but that is only because they don't know things about me that I know about me.
- Sure, I did okay on *this* test, but that is because I lucked out and was only asked the things I *did* know so the next test is likely to wipe me out.

not giving recognitive to good things = disqualifying the positive

Finding ways to move from negative to positive

How do you avoid this trap of disqualifying the positive and focusing on the negative, which is no help at all to you in your studies? Well, remember those metacognitive strategies? Now, is a good time to use them.

Find ways to use some of the strategies below.

- List all the positive things you can think of about your performance, and, if you need affirmation, discuss the list with your teacher.
- Okay, you are not perfect, and there are things you could improve (every one of us can say that); so, take the time and objectively list what you think your weak areas are and then discuss with your teacher or mentor what you can do to improve those weak areas.
- Keep a list of your progress; every time you really learn something new (deeply enough that you will probably not forget it), mark it down in a notebook, and from week to week, see how your list grows.

Think Yourself into Becoming a Language Learning Super Star!

*examining the negative
with a balanced approach = finding the positive*

As soon as you think something negative about yourself, immediately find the positive—and smile! You are good!

Betty Lou Leaver Ph.D.

Labeling and Mislabeling

Closely related to disqualifying the positive is the affective dissonance (a type of cognitive distortion that is more emotion than cognition) of labeling, usually pejoratively, and mislabeling (most pejorative labels *are* mislabels). Sometimes, labeling and mislabeling has been referred to as negative self-talk, but it is more than self-talk. It is a matter of putting yourself into a category—and we are all larger than any category.

It is, of course, human nature to want to label the things around us. We want categories of things for storing information neatly in our brain. We don't really like things that don't fit neatly into a category. In this case, though, it is not things you are labeling—and mislabeling. It is yourself, and that has significant repercussions for learning.

Identifying mislabels

Labeling and mislabeling refers to having to have a tag in order to hang onto something. So, if you look at someone (including yourself) and say that the person you are seeing will be the next president of your organization, you have some tags: success, president, XYZ organization. Into each of these three boxes goes that person's image.

Boxes can have great labels: examples of brilliance, compassionate neighbors, and the like. This, though, is business as usual, healthy thinking, and objective labeling.

What we are talking about as an affective dissonance is a label that is negative and, as such, typically too narrow and nearly always wrong: a mislabel. So, let's say you label someone (including yourself) as a doofus, that image of you or the other person goes into some boxes for storage: dumb, cut-up, failure.

Now, if you have to keep looking for your own label in one of these boxes, pretty soon your mind will convince you that you are the things that appear on the tags for the boxes. Though those negative characteristics very likely do not describe you accurately, after some time, you will believe they do. Then, they start to become reality, and your performance suffers. Unfortunately, when you are down on yourself, it is difficult to move forward or up.

What does being down on yourself look like? Well, have you ever caught yourself thinking or saying any of the following?

- "I am not a good language learner; I don't know why my teachers just do not give up on me."
- "I just can't learn all this vocabulary I am seeing in these authentic articles; I don't have a good enough memory."
- "I can't handle this cross-culture stuff; I know I come across as an 'Ugly American'[11] [or whatever your nationality], because, in truth, I am."

any label = mislabeling
(because we are all larger than one category)

Avoiding the bad labels

So, how do get out of these boxes in which you have mislabeled yourself? Change the label! Start telling yourself that you are a good language learner; if you tell yourself that often enough, you will start believing it, you will be

---

[11] For those reading this book who were not around a few decades ago, *The Ugly American* is the name of a satiric book, written in 1958 by Burdick and reprinted in 2019 by Burdick and Lederer, showing Americans as highly incompetent cross-culturally.

placing yourself in a box for good learners, and your statement will start coming true. We rise to our beliefs! Once you start changing the labels on your boxes, you will see the content (you) differently.

Here are some suggestions:

- Repeat to yourself every time you sit down to study: I can do this; I am a good language learner.
- When you truly cannot remember all the new vocabulary you encounter, especially in authentic readings; think about the methods you are using to internalize the words; if they do not match your preferred learning style, change how you are studying—and when you succeed, change the label: I am a great vocabulary learner.
- Tutor someone else (yes, even if you are not an A+ student); there are always others in an earlier stage of learning than you—and watch what labels your mentee gives you!

positive input = positive labels

Labels are not permanent attachments; if the label is wrong, change it!

Betty Lou Leaver Ph.D.

Anxiety

Everyone experiences anxiety, no matter how capable or how easy a life any person seems to have.[12] Everyone has problems; just scratch the surface. And problems create anxiety.

Generally, the greatest source of anxiety comes from not having the means to resolve a problem even if you know how to resolve it. If you cannot pay rent because your income is too low, of course, you will feel some anxiety.

Classroom anxiety comes from a similar source—except often the lack of means of resolving a problem is a perceived lack, not a real lack. You are nervous about a test because you don't have enough time to study, but you have waited until the last minute so you need to cram. Of course, you feel anxiety. You probably also realize that you did not have to wait until the last minute, and next time you can rectify it.

Some students experience severe test anxiety. That is covered later in the section on tests, but if you cannot wait, flip there now.

Defining anxiety in language learning

Generalized learning anxiety, though, is something somewhat different. It envelopes you like a big gray cloud almost all the time, or at least when you are in class or thinking about class. This is not normal nervousness. It is at best an affective dissonance and at worst something for which you may need professional help.

---

12 Ortman (2015) in *Anxiety Anonymous* suggests that some people actually become dependent upon or addicted to their anxiety. This is a real issue and not one you can solve alone. Professional help is needed for any addiction. What we are talking about in this chapter are the lesser forms of anxiety.

You may be experiencing anxiety if any of the following conditions listed below describe you:

- Do you feel sick to your stomach, light-headed, or nervous when you stand outside the classroom door before class?
- Do you get nervous just thinking about class?
- Do your nerves get in the way of doing your homework?

grey cloud + nausea = anxiety

Avoiding anxiety in language learning

Well, honestly speaking, you probably cannot avoid all anxiety, or you would not be human. There is a range of anxiety from a little to a lot that you can dispel. Then, there is overwhelming anxiety, which probably involves more than just your language classes, which you probably cannot handle alone.

To manage anxiety associated with language learning, try some of these ideas:

- Prepare for your classes and tests well and prepare in advance; do a little learning every day, and you will not have to do a lot on the night of the exam; do a little on your project every day, and you won't have to hurry up and finish it at the last minute and make mistakes that you could have caught.
- Complete your assignments early, lay them away, and go back to them in a few hours or a day; this lets you look at them with fresh eyes to find mistakes and reinforces the information through repetition to en-

ter long-term memory (just in case it is not already there).
- Get together with your classmates for fun and study; working together takes a lot of stress out of learning.
- Analyze what is making you nervous (likely something you have not been able to understand in your lessons); if that knowledge alone is not enough to help you, talk to your teacher about getting some help or tutoring.

knowledge + preparation = less classroom anxiety

Determine the source of your anxiety; then, do something about it—prepare better, soothe yourself through appropriate positive self-talk, or, where needed, get some professional help.

Betty Lou Leaver Ph.D.

Tactics and Strategies

Betty Lou Leaver Ph.D.

When you are struggling to learn on a foreign language, it may feel like you are on a battlefield. You are, in a way. You have an objective. You are out to conquer something: the language. But that is as far as one might be able to stretch the image. Most programs teach language for peace, and some of the best cross-cultural bridge builders are foreign language students who have achieved the capacity to use the language for work and leisure.

How most people reach that point is through good language learning tactics and strategies. Tactics refer to ways of accomplishing something in the short term; they are simple and have narrow objectives. They are actions. Strategies are how one goes about accomplishing a goal for the long term: they can have greater breadth and applicability. They are plans.

In language learning, strategies and tactics play a role as well. Language learners need a plan, and they need actions to accomplish that plan. (Note: most books and articles on learning strategies lump tactics and strategies together, and there really is no reason not to in most cases. In the case of this book, we separate them for greater clarification.)

The next section looks at some of the struggles that can come along with language learning, as well as the kinds of goals that are typically sent. For each kind of struggle and goal, specific representative tactics and strategies are suggested. If you want (and you should want) more comprehensive information on any of these topics, you should consult some of the very good books about these topics, the complete details of which are in the reference list at the back of this book. Specifically,

- for how to be a good language learner, check out *Lessons from Good Language Learners* (Carol Griffiths), *How to Be a More Successful Language Learner* (Rubin & Thompson), *Success with Foreign Languages: Seven[13] Who Achieved It and What Worked for Them* (Stevick), *Passport to the World: Learning to Communicate in a Foreign Language* (Leaver, Dubinsky, & Champine), *Achieving Success in Second Language Acquisition* (Leaver, Ehrman, & Shekhtman), and *What Works: Helping Students Reach Near-Native Second-Language Competence* (Coalition of Distinguished Language Centers);

- for deepening your knowledge of grammar, check out the Olivia Hill Publishers series of books of English grammar for students of various languages—I have included their Italian version (*English Grammar for Students of Italian* by Adorni and Primorac) in the reference list, but they have these books for many languages so you should check for your target language;

- for deepening your knowledge of vocabulary, you

---

[13] Here I will give away a secret since the late Earl Stevick and the late Madeline Ehrman, both of whom were friends of mine, cannot. I am sure both would not mind if I divulge the secret that they maintained for almost three decades: Gwen, one of the seven learners that Earl describes, is Madeline.

do not need suggestions, you just need to read, read, read, and spend a lot of time listening to your foreign language;

- for learning strategies, check out *Teaching and Researching Language Learning Strategies* (Oxford)[14]
- for dealing with errors, there is not much literature available and none I can refer you to—most of what is available is for teachers and even that is limited, but hopefully, the suggestions in this book will help and perhaps, as a result of your becoming very good at managing errors, you will write your own book on the topic;
- for developing independence in learning, check out *Learner Strategies for Learner Autonomy: Planning and Implementing Learner Strategy Training for Language Learners* (Wenden);
- for study abroad recommendations, check out *Preparing to Study Abroad: Learning to Cross Cultures* (Duke).

While I would like to present a comprehensive list of everything you need to know on the topic of tactics and strategies, space does not allow. As you can see, whole books can be written on these topics and have been. Probably all are in your library. All are available online. Take advantage of the guidance they can give you.

---

[14] Please note that this book goes well beyond strategies for improving reading, writing, listening, and speaking. It includes work on memory, compensation (managing when you don't know the words), and metacognition. This is a book you should have on your shelf and in your hands if you want to succeed at language learning.

Betty Lou Leaver Ph.D.

Thinking Like a Good Language Learner

Extensive studies, beginning in the 1970s, have been conducted about what makes a good language learner (Reeves, 2019; Rubin & Thompson, 1994; Stevick, 1990; among many others). From those studies, we have learned many of the common traits and actions that help learners succeed at language learning. If you are interested in learning more about the results of these studies than there is room to include here, check out the list of books recommended in the previous pages.

Strategies

If you think of strategies as long-term plans to reach ultimate objectives, then those strategies need to focus on bringing your traits (attitudes and behaviors) into alignment with the traits of good language learners. These are not things you do; these are things you become.

You will need to assess who you are and what you have already become. What traits do you already have in common with good language learners? A lot? Great! But you can always find more. Only a few? Well, you know what you have to do.

Below are some of the strategies that many learners who ultimate achieved success have used.

- Develop courage: learning language is risky business; you have to speak in front of your classmates, and you will sound funny, at least at first; you will not always get the grammar or vocabulary correct because (1) you do not know it and have to guess (better to circumlocute, guessing is not a precise science), (2) you learned it wrong, or (3) you experience a retrieval error; all of this can make you feel awkward in front of peers so develop courage.

- Develop metacognitive control: learning to think about thinking automatically and always will allow you to steer through rough waters and smooth ones because you can objectify your experiences, owning them and not letting them own you.
- Routinize good study habits: once you know what the good study habits are (changes are you know already and have known since elementary school), you need to make them automatic reactions.
- Develop good observation skills: if you want to improve, you need to be aware of how you are performing; if you want to emulate native speakers, you need to notice what they do.
- Be curious: curiosity may kill cats, but it will bring life to your learning experience.
- Increase your creativity: all of us are born with a flair for creativity, but school experiences that force you into being just like everyone else can send creativity into hiding; work on bringing out your creativity.
- Use what you know to good avail: much of language learning is not entirely new—perhaps some of the grammar parallels your native language or another language you have studied, and as you gain knowledge of your new language, you will be able to use what you already know to figure out new information, especially once you understand word-building and grammar patterns.
- Develop greater patience: language learning takes time; those ads that say if you buy a particular book you will speak like a diplomat in 30 days are disingenuous; diplomats spend six months to two years in full-time training (depending upon the language).

Copy-catting good language learners = becoming a good language learner

Tactics

Those are great goals you may think, but how can you get there? What tactics or actions will help?

Below are some activities that fit with the strategies recommended above.

- Develop Courage:
    - Courage does not mean not being afraid; it means doing something in spite of being afraid.
    - Just do it, whatever it is (participating in a role play, reading a poem aloud, guessing at the meaning of a word or how to form one).
    - Realize that the first time doing anything that you are worried will cause others to laugh at you will be the hardest; you will develop both skill and greater courage as you "just do it" again and again.
- Develop metacognitive control:
    - In the classroom, pay attention to what you are doing.
    - Figure out what works for you.
    - If you don't understand something or fall behind, don't panic but rather put in extra effort or get help to catch up.
    - Monitor your progress and reward yourself when appropriate.
- Routinize good study habits:
    - Do homework while you are still rested.

- Go beyond minimal effort and do more on your class project or write a story in your language to share with the class or teacher.
- After you finish your assigned homework, review previous lessons to keep old language fresh.
  - Find ways to use your language outside the classroom.
  - Learn something extra every day.
  - To help you routinize these things, put times on your calendar and a checklist on your desk.
- Develop good observation skills:
  - Pay attention to errors you make that are corrected by your teacher or that you see by comparing your response to an authentic text.
  - Look for patterns in the language in how words are formed and related to each other and how the grammar works.
  - Look for non-verbal cues that show, beyond what someone is saying, how they say it—facial expressions, head movements, body movements, and the like can help you figure out meaning when you "don't have a clue."
- Be curious:
  - Ask a lot of questions.
  - When you read something on a new topic, look up more information on line.
- Increase your creativity:
  - If you have a penchant for it, write short stories or poems, using language you have just learned; it will help store it in memory better.

- Improvise when you do not know how to say something: use paraphrasing and circumlocution, or even change the topic (if/when you can) to one you do know.
- Figure out yourself and how you learn and move toward adapting your lessons to the way in which you learn best (the next section in this book should help you with that).

- Use what you know:
  - When encountering something new, check your memory for similar things you have recently learned in the language.
  - Use context to figure out meaning.
  - Use your own background knowledge of the topic to figure out what you do not understand, e.g., is the topic about science, and do you already know the scientific principles in the text you are reading? Or perhaps you are reading about some oddities in elections in the target country and you have already read about some of them in your home town newspaper—use that information to advantage.
  - If you do not have any background information on the topic, research the topic online in your native language in order to understand the concepts; then, all you have to deal with is a set of foreign words and perhaps some new grammatical forms.
  - When all else fails, you do know how to use logic, right? Use logic to figure out what something cannot mean so that whatever possibility remains is very likely what it does mean.

- When you speak, be conservative; don't try to be as erudite as you are in your native language, which forces you into a lot of guessing and paraphrasing; rather, use what you do know to speak accurately, if simply. Sophisticated expression will come later as you grow in proficiency.
- Develop greater patience:
  - Nothing contributes more to language acquisition than time on task, so spend as much time as possible with your language.
  - Keep in mind when you think you are making no progress that language has to marinate and that language proficiency development takes time—so give yourself time, patiently.

taking frequent little actions
over time = making big gains over time

For every good-learner strategy, there is a set of good learner tactics; use good-learner tactics to become a good learner.

Deepening Your Knowledge

No matter how you look at it, if you are going to get better at your language, you will need to broaden and deepen your knowledge. More words, more sophisticated words, more complex sentences, greater grammatical control, and a growing understanding of the culture are all important.

This is not what we call proficiency, and someone with less knowledge but more skill at using what he or she knows can actually be more proficient in a language than someone who actually knows less. However, a broad vocabulary, a deep understanding of grammar, and a wide acceptance of cultural differences (and the knowledge of those differences) can set you up to become highly proficient once you develop the language skills you will need (reading, writing, listening, and speaking).

Strategies

So, how do you go about getting this broad vocabulary, deep understanding of grammar, and extensive knowledge of culture? What kinds of strategies will help you achieve these long-term objectives?

Use the guidelines for developing your strategic approach.

- Vocabulary: You will need broad vocabulary for every day things, but for professional things, not so much; think about what professional topics will you be using in your career—that is the vocabulary you need to work on acquiring, not vocabulary for nuclear physics (unless you are a physicist), astrometrics (unless you plan to work with or in space), or any vocabulary that you do not know in English (though sometimes it happens because of cultural differences, literary fiction that you may read, or odd conversations you may happen into that you will learn vocabulary in your target language that you do not know in your native language—it is not extremely common, but it happens. (In languages that do not use the Latin alphabet, in addition to the sounds of words, you will need to learn how the words are written, and in languages that use gender markers, you need to know the gender of the nouns you learn.)

- Grammar: You will need all the basic grammar for the language—how to express how words relate to each other and sentential functions, how to indicate the time in which something has occurred, how words are formed

- Culture: Knowing words and grammar is not enough if you do not know how and where to use them appropriately. So, acquiring a strong sense of culture should indeed be one of your strategies for language improvement. You do not have to become a cultural chameleon. You do not have to have a goal of passing for a native speaker; realistically, a blue-eyed blond studying Chinese will never be able to pass for being Chinese regardless the level of proficiency attained. What you do need to do is determine the kind of relationship you want to have with the culture—to be able to do business as a foreigner, to work together as a partner on some kind of project or in some kind of organization, to enroll at a university, to conduct research with colleagues, or whatever else dream or need brought you to the language course in the first place. That desired relationship will set the parameters for how well you need to know the culture and how extensively.

Think Yourself into Becoming a Language Learning Super Star!

*insightful analysis of needs
and desires = development of good strategies*

Tactics

Once you have completed an insightful analysis of your needs and established your strategies for acquisition of vocabulary, grammar, and cross-cultural competence, you need to figure out what methods (tactics) you will need to reach your objective. (These tactics are often listed as learning strategies.)

Below are some ways to think about how to approach your tasks tactically:

- Increase your vocabulary:[15]
    - Avoid being overwhelmed by long lists of words to learn (unless you are in a program that gives a daily or weekly vocabulary list—I hope we are past that nowadays) by keeping a personal dictionary of the words that you want to remember for personal reasons, such as words that you have

---

15 I absolutely do not recommend what worked like a charm for me in learning Russian as a young soldier at the Defense Language Institute. I bought two copies of a Russian-English dictionary and cut out all the words (two copies since I needed the words on both the front and the back of the page). Every day I would spend a half-hour randomly pulling out words from the dictionary bucket and, if I knew them, adding them to my bucket. Gradually, my bucket got quite full, and the dictionary bucket became less full. By the end of the year-long course, I knew more vocabulary than anyone in my class: thousands of words. That did help me tremendously on the final proficiency exam, which was wide-ranging and not based only on class activities. This would be an unwieldy and unsuccessful tactic for most learners. If you are like me, however—a concrete-random learner (hands-on and non-sequential) with near-eidetic memory and a background in structural linguistics, go for it!

needed for presentations, words that you use all the time in your native language, and words you have come across that simply appeal to you and you know therefore that you will find an opportunity to use them.

- To remember words short-term (with continued use, they will stay with you long-term), repeat them every opportunity you get. I have personally found the 3-3-3 rule very helpful. Using a new word or expression deliberately three times over three days in three different contexts means that word has become mine. I don't have to work anymore at learning it. Try 3-3-3, and see if it works for you, too!

- Account for your sensory preferences in how you go about learning new words: if you learn best through your eyes, read a lot of articles on the topic associated with the vocabulary you want or need to learn. If you learn best by using your ears, listen to a lot of broadcasts, or more fun, movies on the topic associated with the words you want to learn. If you depend upon movement to learn, get physically involved from playing (usually children's) games in the language that target the words of interest to you to computer games (at least, your hands are moving) to acting out words (Charades, anyone?). If you really do not have a preference, then do all three; even if you do have a preference, move on from your initial mode of acquiring the words to using, hearing, or reading the words in a non-preferred style. The more senses you use to acquire vocabulary, the more avenues you will have for recalling the words.

- Grammar:
    - Grammar is probably best learned "in the wild"[16] or, in other words, in context. Learning grammar through decontextualized rules parallels the task of pushing a rock up a hill. Ultimately, you might make it, though not without many rollbacks. Grammar does not occur in real life in isolation so learning it in isolation does not make a lot of sense, yet nearly every textbook presents grammar in this fashion.
    - If you are not taught grammar in context, then go hunting "in the wild" for examples of the grammar you are studying—in articles, movies, broadcast, TV shows, novels, short stories, letters, editorials, whatever you can find wherever you can find it. The Internet is a big help in tracking down these examples.
    - To remember new grammar, associate it with grammar you already know. Perhaps it parallels English or another language you have studied. Perhaps it builds on something you have already studied in your target language, an example in Russian being the relationship between past tense (usually met earlier in context and textbooks) and participles (usually met later).
    - To understand grammar and even predict it, ex-

---

16   Dr. Philip Johnson, an American with near-native control of Arabic and an outstanding Arabic instructor at the Defense Language Institute, coined this phrase. He never taught grammar that was not embedded in some form of communication: articles, literature of any sort, recorded conversations, broadcasts, movies, etc. His students always tested among the best of the best in the Arabic program.

panding your ability to speak and write grammatically correct, look for patterns. Test them out by applying them in your writing and conversation and see if they work; most of the time, they will.

- Culture:
  - Area studies publications can help you understand the historical and social facts and statistics about the culture you are studying, and, fortunately, a great many experts have written a great many books about almost any culture. Google your culture: you will find them. Happily, you can find some very helpful language-learner-focused area studies materials, paid for with taxpayer dollars (meaning that they can be obtained by you for free) on the Defense Language Institute Foreign Language Center's website. Use the URL: www.dliflc.edu. Then, look for products.
  - Other kinds of cultural materials look more at the everyday side of culture[17] in various countries. Sometimes, words and expressions are associated with everyday culture; sometimes not. Either way, not knowing these things, even if your linguistic skills are superb, reduces your ability to interact

---

17 Dr. James Bernhardt, an educational administrator at the Foreign Service Institute, calls this "gee whiz" culture, meaning that this aspect of culture includes the kinds of everyday things that two cultures do differently, such that when you encounter some aspect of it, you are likely to say, "Gee, whiz, I would not have done it that way" or "gee, whiz, who would have thought that." An example of gee whiz culture is baby showers. They are expected in the United States; they are not done in Russia—could bring bad luck to celebrate a baby's birth before the baby is born. Another example is bringing flowers to someone is good in the United States. It is also good in Russia, but only if you bring an odd number of them. Gee whiz! Who would have thought...!

- In some cultures, words and sentence structure can reflect a different way of thinking that is not really noticeable until you pay attention to it. For example., in English, we say, "I am a doctor," but in Arabic and Russian, one says, "I doctor" and in German "I am doctor." Perhaps a Russian example can better demonstrate a cultural mindset difference. In English, one says, "Can you tell me the time?" In Russian, one says, "Will you not tell me the time?" In Russian, the negative used in this way shows politeness; to some speakers of English, it seems odd or even rude.[18]

- These differences do not apply only to street talk, kitchen conversations, and chit-chat among friends. They also can play an important role in business as well. Several books have been written on this topic—do a search for them. An older one that I like for its simplicity is *Kiss, Bow, or Shake Hands* (Morrison & Conaway, 2006).

- When you notice something odd culturally that does not make sense to you, check it out on the Internet, from a book, or with a native speaker. You may find something of great interest or tremendous value.

---

18 There are so many such cases of negative expressions used to show politeness that one of my Russian students once commented to me, "Wow, the Russians really have a negative view of the world!" Well, they don't, but with literal translations, it can seem so. That is why understanding cultural differences for what they are is so important.

Betty Lou Leaver Ph.D.

*using methods that fit you
personally = reaching your own strategic goals sooner*

Deep and broad acquisition of vocabulary, grammar, and cross-cultural competence represent the trifecta in the race for language proficiency!

Sharpening Your Skills

Sharpening your skills means becoming better at reading, writing, listening, and speaking. (For this book, we will leave translation and interpretation out of the equation; those are special skills for individuals who have already gained considerable proficiency in the language, but if your goal is to be a translator or interpreter, yes, indeed, you will have another set of skills to sharpen.)

Your strategies for sharpening your skills are going to look differently depending upon your reason for studying your language. Your tactics for reaching your strategic goals, commonly also considered learning strategies,[19] will also differ depending upon your goal.

Strategies

Before you can decide how to go about improving your reading, writing, listening, and speaking, you need to identify to what extent you need each of these skills and how well you have to be able to use it. That directly relates to two things: (1) why you took the course and (2) what you

---

[19] Most of the literature, including the very best literature and research on learning strategies do not separate strategies and tactics the way I have done in this book. For most intents and purposes, there is no real need to do so. The teacher who is trying to help the student apply more strategies and more pertinent strategies does not need to think long-term, not really. The focus is on immediate improvement and developing strategies that the learner can always have access to. For learners reading this book for whom language learning success extends beyond the current course or even beyond any course, the focus is both long-term and short-term. I chose, rather arbitrarily, though quite in keeping with dictionary and military definitions, the terms *strategies* and *tactics* to delineate what is long-term and what is short-term. The former is for planning; the latter is for studying. This division, I believe, helps identify the purpose of actions that generally carry the label, *learning strategy*.

plan to do with the language in your life. Those can be the same thing, or they can be very different things. Perhaps you took the course because your job requires it, but you have a 5-year commitment to that job and don't plan to use the language again. Or, perhaps after your job commitment, you would like to teach the language. Or, perhaps you took the language because you married a native speaker of the language and want to be able to communicate better with your spouse and in-laws. All of these will result in different strategic goals.

Below are some guidelines to help your planning process.

- Reading: Your reading goal will depend upon your answers to the following questions:
  - What kinds of things will you be reading once you have attained your skill-level goal? Will it be standard daily fare like newspapers? Or, are you into literature, even planning a major in the literature of one or more of the countries where your language is spoken? Or, are there professional documents you will need to be able to read for a job requirement? Clearly, then, you will need to develop strategies to handle whichever genre you will be reading—and all have quite a different structure and set of expressions in most languages.
  - Is one of your goals to become a translator? (Okay, so we cannot completely omit the question of translation and interpretation in this book.) If so, are you planning on a specific field—law, military, literary, medical (the list is almost endless, of course)? In that case, you will need to develop deep expertise in the vocabulary, expressions, and content of that field. Alternatively, do you just

want to be able to do some translation to bring in some moonlighting funds? In that case, you will need to develop quite a breadth of vocabulary and expressions in a number of fields but will not likely be able to develop depth in all of them; perhaps you can single out 3-4 fields that are the most interesting to you.

- Writing:
  - Writing is a skill that many students dislike—and insist that they will never need. Don't be so sure! You may end up having to write notes to your host family if you end up on study abroad. Or, if you marry a native speaker, very likely you will be writing more than you had planned. Some jobs require writing, too; if so, figure that kind of writing into your goals.[20]
  - If you have a desire to become either a translator or interpreter, you will need to be able to write. If you are translating into your foreign language, you definitely will need writing skills!
  - Do you want to be a good reader? Then, you need good writing skills. Writing will help you understand language expression and text structure much more thoroughly than just a lot of reading.
- Listening: Your listening goal will depend upon your answers to the following questions:

---

[20] A common job as an intern abroad or in working abroad is to copy-edit/proofread for a publishing house. In that case, you will need very good writing skills and a good knowledge of grammar. If you have lesser language skills and are hired for editing books in your native language, you will need good writing skills in your native language. With the exception of grammar and stylistic differences, good writing skills do transfer from language to language.

- What kinds of things will you be listening to once you have attained your skill-level goal? Will it be standard daily fare like soap operas, newscasts, and friends (or spouse)? Or, are you into movies, even planning a major in the film studies of one or more of the countries where your language is spoken? Or, are there professional kinds of oral texts you will need to be able to understand for a job requirement? Clearly, then, you will need to develop strategies to handle whichever genre you will be listening to—and all have quite a different structure and set of expressions in most languages.

- Is one of your goals to become an interpreter? If so, are you planning on a specific field—diplomacy, medical, treaty management (the list is almost endless, of course)? In that case, you will need to develop deep expertise in the vocabulary, expressions, and content of that field. Alternatively, do you just want to be able to do some interpretation to bring in some moonlighting funds? In that case, you will need to develop quite a breadth of vocabulary and expressions in a number of fields but will not likely be able to develop depth in all of them; perhaps you can single out 3-4 fields that are the most interesting to you.

- Speaking: Your speaking goal will depend upon your answers to the following questions:

  - Speaking is a skill that some learners in professional courses that are focused on the ability to translate or interpret from the foreign language into the native language (the most common combination) insist that they will never need. Don't be so sure! If someone knows that you know a language and is with someone who speaks only that language, you may be expected to step up and help out. That has happened to me more often than I can probably recall. In one case, I interpreted for speakers of Polish, Russian, Italian, and Spanish on an air flight to Frankfurt that was turned back with mechanical problems—and that unexpectedly earned me a free first-class ticket! I have experienced the need for my speaking skill many, many times. There are also cases where help is needed and not available—if only you had learned to speak the language!

- If you have a desire to become an interpreter, you will need to be able to speak your target language even if your preference and intention is to interpret only into your native language. You will need to make arrangements with, answer questions from, and otherwise communicate with native speakers. If you are interpreting into your foreign language, you definitely will need really good speaking skills!

- Do you want to be a good listener? Then, you need good speaking skills. Speaking will help you understand language expressions and text structure much more thoroughly than just a lot of listening will—and faster. When we can make the sounds, we can hear them better. When we learn to use proper intonation patters in the foreign language, we are not put off when we hear them.[21]

---

[21] Hopman and MacDonald (2018) found that students with better speaking skills outperformed all other students on listening tasks.

*identify what you want to do
with your language = shape your learning more effectively*

Tactics

Once you have completed an insightful analysis of your needs and established your strategies for acquisition of the four language skills, you need to figure out what methods (tactics) you will need to reach your objective. The tactics may be quite fluid, flowing among the four skills since writing supports reading and speaking, reading supports listening and speaking, speaking supports listening and writing, and listening supports speaking and reading. You cannot pull these four apart; they are best friends.

If you want to become more skilled, you have to be wise in how you go about building those skills. Listening "harder," just like "studying harder," is not good advice. What does "harder" mean? Most people cannot answer that question, other than to say to do more. More of the same, though, rarely helps. Study, listen, read, write, and speak more wisely—that is what will help you improve. What "wiser" means you *can* define. Those are your tactics.

Listed below are some ways to think about how to approach your tasks tactically. Pick those that work best with your strategic goals. If you find yourself wanting more, read one of the books listed in the reference section on learning strategies.

- Reading:
  - At the sentence or paragraph level, if you have trouble understanding a complicated sentence unwind it and put it into your native-language structure. In English, this would be SVO. Find the

subject, a simple noun, not the modifiers. Then, find the main *verb*, the simple verb, not the whole verb phrase. Then, find the *object* of the verb if there is one. So, the sentence, *the kind and compassionate president of the well-known and highly respected Save the Dogs Foundation proudly and formally hung a silver framed picture of members of the organization who had been recognized by the city council for their great work* becomes *president hung picture*—a very clear, concise encapsulation of the content of the sentence. After that, you can go back and fill in all those modifiers, figuring out what the individual words mean as you do so, including the relative clause (which can also be broken down the same way). Once you have the correct skeletal sentence, you really have the key you need to unlock the sentence, paragraph, or text.

- At the text level, find the topic sentence. So, you have been reading for a while, right? Think about how you go about reading. Do you pay attention to the first sentence of the first paragraph and use that to figure out what the article was going to be about? If you are a native speaker of English, you do. Will this work effectively in your target language? For most European languages, yes. For languages like Arabic, no. So, if the approach you use for your native language works in your foreign language, use it. If you have learned that your language organizes text differently, approach the text the same way a native speaker would. Perhaps that is to skim the first couple of pages until you get to the topic sentence. Or, perhaps, reading the ending will tell you about the beginning. If you don't know, ask your teacher—your teacher knows. If you do not have a teacher, ask your mentor or any native speaker who is helping you—they know, too.

- Scope out the story. Find details that support the topic sentence. Start out by scanning for those details. Then, skim the rest of text to get a general idea of what the story is about. Then, read the whole article with the topic sentence and whatever details you have in mind. Try to figure out the vocabulary and grammar you do not know through logic, comparing it with what you do know, breaking the words into their component parts, and using context as to what the words "should" mean. Only then, resort to dictionary help. The more you can do on our own now, the more you will be able to do later. The more you rely on a dictionary for all your help, the more you will be stuck with having to use the dictionary later.

- Look at the bigger picture. Texts can deliver factual information, directly or indirectly deliver an opinion, or express irony or satire. Texts have differing purposes: to inform, to entertain, or to persuade. Ask questions to figure that out. *What* is the purpose of the text you are reading? *Who* wrote the article? (Read about the author on the Internet, in Wikipedia, or in other publications by him or her.) *For whom* was the text written? *Why*? Figuring out why is called "reading between the lines." When was the text written, what was going on in politics or society at the time and how might this relate to the text? This is called reading beyond the text.

- Read out loud. You saw right. Reading out loud is looked down upon nowadays as a waste of time (and, in class, some learners are embarrassed when asked to read out loud), but reading out loud will do two things for you: (1) if you are someone who learns by hearing, it will help you understand the words better, and (2) if you are a visual learner, you will need to read aloud with someone who can correct your pronunciation since visual learners often do not "hear" how words sound and then, though they can understand what they read, they cannot understand what they hear—you don't want to end up with that dilemma.
- Writing:
  - Use models. Whatever level of proficiency you are at, models exist. Some may be teacher-prepared student materials. Others may be very simple stories. Yet others, when you are ready, may be professional documents, real literature, or other texts meant for native speakers. When you use models instead of dictionaries, you are more likely to get the grammar, expressions, and sentence/text structure right. Language learners who have reached near-native levels of proficiency report that they pretty much exclusively use models.
  - Perfect your understanding of genre. While you will need to be at a pretty strong proficiency level to do this, once you are ready, practicing genre shifts will quickly and greatly increase your writing skill. So, for example, take a newspaper article and rewrite it as a personal letter; then, rewrite it again as if it were a novel. When you can do that

easily, you will have made serious progress in acquiring writing skills.

- Listening:
  - Focus on what you know. At early levels, there may be many words that fly right past you. As scary as that seems, let them go. It is not useful to catch words if you don't know what they mean. Listen instead for the words you do know.
  - Listen for key words. Once you have practiced focusing on what you know, you can start picking out from them the words that seem to have special importance. If you are listening to a weather broadcast, then the key words would be related to weather. Actually, that parallels what native speakers do. They do not listen to every word; they would get bogged down if they did. They pick up on the key words, and the other words fall in line because they know the templates, or scripts.
  - Rely on the script—and learn as many scripts as you can. Scripts are words that always appear in texts of various types: a wide range of news reports, science reports, and so on. In the case of the weather broadcast, the script may start out *date* it will be *how* and *how* in the *time*. (*Today it will be warm and sunny in the morning.*) The words in italics are the key words: *today, warm, sunny, morning*. The scripted words *it will be, and, in the*, are always there; they fade into the background for native speakers (who could call them up if needed because they are always the same). So, too, they should fade into the background for you for efficient and native-like listening.

- Build the story. Frequently, there will be many words that you do not know. Don't be concerned. Listen for the words you do know. When strung together, what story might they tell?

- Use background knowledge. If you think you are listening to a text about tourists picking cotton in Yalta (an example taken from an actual class I once taught), give it the commonsense test. Do tourists pick cotton? Does cotton grow in Yalta? In both cases, the answer is no. So, you are misunderstanding something. Listen again! (By the way, the greater your background knowledge, the more you will automatically understand. So, read everything you can about the target culture.)

- Where you can, control how you receive the oral input. That is easy with digital input; just replay it. Likewise, when talking to a native speaker, control your interlocutor. If you miss something, ask for a repeat either directly, or better, subtly, as in "what did you mean by that?" rather than "repeat, please."

- Increase the frequency. The best way, regardless of or in addition to the tactics your use, listen a lot, with regular frequency. The very best way to learn to listen well is to listen frequently and regularly.

- Speaking[22]

---

[22] One of the best books I have seen for teaching rapid acquisition of good speaking skills is *How to Improve Your Foreign Language Immediately* (Shekhtman, 2013). I have included a few of Shekhtman's tools here and highly recommend reading his book to learn about the remainder of the tools if you find the islands and simplification tools helpful.

- Models. As with writing, the best way to speak correctly is not trying to string together words from a dictionary, using memorized grammar rules. It is to follow a model where that has already been done, and all you have to do is change the players, the actions, the topic. Dialogues (as much as they are not popular for teaching these days) and role plays can provide these models for you.[23]

- Islands. Shekhtman (2013) refers to memorized short and medium-length texts that you will often be saying, for example, your biographical information. Memorizing these texts to the point of automaticity means that you do not need to think about them while speaking, and your speech will be correct.

- Simplification. One of the biggest mistakes learners make when speaking at lower levels of proficiency is try to be as erudite in the target language as in their native language. Of course, that is not possible, and the attempt usually ends up with the learner doing much direct translation from native to target language, with the result often being unintelligible. By using only what you know, you will end up with simple—but accurate—language.

- Find opportunities to speak. As with other skills, the more you use the skill, the better you become at using the skill. Find opportunities to speak with native speakers as often as you can. Help the emigrants in your community to learn the ways of life or help them with a problem (children at school,

---

[23] Conversely, just as reading can help writing by providing models, listening can improve speaking by providing models.

trying to rent an apartment, whatever they might need). Attend literary events arranged for native speakers. The list is limited only to the resources of your community and your imagination. (And there are always online friendships via Skype and online speaking partner programs.)

avoid confusion from the abundance of learning strategies lists = pick tactics that meet your learning strategies goals

The four skills—reading, writing, listening, and speaking—are best friends, supporting each other. Pull one away, and the support weakens, so give fair attention to all.

Betty Lou Leaver Ph.D.

Making Errors

Good learners make mistakes and errors. Lots of them. They are risk-takers, and risk-takers take missteps. An important difference between good learners and poor learners is that good learners embrace mistakes and learn from them whereas poor students are afraid to make mistakes, try to avoid them, generally make more from nervousness, and end up both speaking less and failing to develop good speaking skills.

In gaining control over your mistakes, understanding the difference between mistake and error is critical. *Mistakes* occur when you produce something that is not correct by accident; you know how it should be said or written, but you experience a brain glitch so that out slips a misspelling, a wrong form, or a wrong word. *Errors* occur when you don't know how something should be said or written, and you guess wrong.

Both mistakes and errors are a natural part of developing greater proficiency. The greatest difficulty, though, is that you cannot adjust your speech if you do not know you are making an error. Therefore, you need the help of your teacher or a native speaker.

Strategies

You do have some control over how you use the help of a native speaker. You also have control over how you react to making mistakes. This may be an area where you have to become your own best motivator and cheerleader.

Below are some strategies to think about.

- Decide that risk-taking will be the new you, and that by the end of the course, you will be almost comfortable with making mistakes.

- Determine that you will track your errors, not in order to reduce the number but in order to increase the complexity of the language where they occur. Be happy to see your errors being reflected in more sophisticated language than earlier.
- While it is impossible to eliminate mistakes completely, make a plan (a list of tactics) that will reduce the number of mistakes you make with the intent of being wiser about mistakes before the course ends.

errors from risk-taking = good learner

Tactics

If you make errors, you need your teacher's help. Think about how you might go about getting it. If you make mistakes, that is on you. You need to put some tactics into place that will help you reduce your mistakes.[24]

Here are some tactics that might help.

- Pay attention. Errors occur when you fail to pay attention to the forms of language (spelling, endings, particles) while you are learning them. If you fail to learn them correctly, then you are bound to make errors. By focusing deliberately on all aspects of words, grammar, and expressions when you first meet them, you are less likely to make errors later.

---

[24] Learning style preferences play a role in who makes mistakes the most. Synoptic learners tend to make a lot of mistakes whereas ectenic learners make many fewer. The two kinds of learners, described in the next section, have different strengths and weaknesses. In the area of mistakes, the synoptic learners are the ones who struggle the most. For more information about learning style differences, check out works by Ehrman and Leaver (2002), Leaver (1997, 2019), and Ehrman, Leaver, and Oxford (2003).

- Monitor yourself. Mistakes occur when you fail to pay attention to the forms of the language as you speak or write. If this happens a lot,[25] you may need to build a monitor. You can do this by rewriting your essays once you teacher has corrected them so that you practice writing correctly. (Seems dull, but it will improve the accuracy of your writing.) If you are making a presentation or doing a role play, record it on your cell phone, find your mistakes (don't worry about finding your own errors—you can't; your teacher will need to point them out), confirm with your teacher, then re-do the presentation as many times as it takes to speak without mistakes. After a while, you will start to sense when you are about to make a mistake and stop yourself. That may make you seem like you are speaking worse, with a lot of false starts. Ultimately, your brain will "get it" and stop you from making the mistake before you start to say it.

- Avoid direct translation. Errors happen when you try to reproduce something in the foreign language that you know in your native language but have not yet learned in the foreign language so you try to say the same thing in the same way through direct translation—and find out it is wrong after the fact.[26] Instead of trying to translate, paraphrase. (If you know a related language, e.g. you are studying Portuguese but already speak Spanish, chances of surviving a direct translation are higher.)

---

25 This happens a lot more frequently with synoptic learners (see the next section of this book).

26 This happens a lot more frequently with ectenic learners (see the next section of this book).

pay attention and/or monitor = cleaner speech

Do not fear errors and mistakes; fix them.

Individual Traits That Affect How Well You Learn—and How to Manage Them

Betty Lou Leaver Ph.D.

This section of the book could be much larger because there are many, many ways in which people differ from each other. So, since it is not possible to reproduce here what has already been published in dozens of books, only an overview is given along with references to works that can take you as deeply into personal traits as you would like.

When we are talking about individual traits, the most important thing to remember is that you are unique—and finding the unique things about you that can get in the way of learning or contributing positively to it is a matter of sifting through a lot of variables. The bottom line, though, is that only you know you. Many different ways of looking at yourself are presented here. Find those that fit you most perfectly and discard the rest.

Use the guidance given to other learners like you, whether that be a preference in how you receive information (orally, visually, or through action), a particular personality type trait, a learning style that throws you into a style war[27] with your classmates or teacher. You are unique, but for every unique trait, there are others like you with that special trait, and you can learn from what has helped others like you in the past.

---

[27] *Style war* is a term coined by Rebecca Oxford, Madeline Ehrman, and Roberta Lavine to describe what happens in classrooms where the teaching style is the polar opposite of a student's learning style (Oxford et al., 1991).

Sensory Preferences

Sensory preferences refer to the ways in which you perceive information, i.e. how you take in new information. While there are tests to figure this out (e.g., Barsch, 1995), you probably already know which sensory preference works for you; reading, listening, or writing things down. These are considered the three major sensory preferences.[28]

The wisdom is that you should use your sensory preference while learning new information. If your sensory preference is not accounted for in the classroom, then it is essential for your success to get the same information in the form that you need it in order to learn it well.

Using a non-preferred style for review of material either in class or at home is fine. In fact, it is good. It will stretch you, cause you to develop a set of strategies for another preference, and make you more flexible in the long run. This is important because language is oral and written; you cannot opt out of either form.

Visual learners

Visual learners learn through sight. Reading is a learning mechanism for them. Flashcards can work, too, depending upon the type of visual learner: one who learns by seeing words or one who learns by seeing images. Flashcards are probably not the best way to learn vocabulary although most visual learners swear by them because they provide no context for the words and there is no easy way then to use the words when you need them. Better to use reading texts.

---

28 There are others, such as haptic (touching) and olfactory (smelling), but visual, auditory, and motor are the most pertinent to language learning.

Dealing with listening texts may be a problem. A transcript, if you can get one, of a show, movie, podcast, or conversation can definitely help. At first, listen and read at the same time. When your skills get better, read first, then listen. Finally, listen first, then check understanding by reading.

books = tools of visual learners

Auditory learners

If you are an auditory learner, your listening ability will likely outstrip your reading ability. Auditory learners come in two varieties: aural and oral.

Aural learners learn by listening. If you are an aural learner, you may need to ask your teacher or native speaker to read the newspaper articles assigned for homework aloud for you so that you can record them. Or, if they are read aloud in class, go ahead and record them. In using these texts where you have auditory support for the text, read them in three ways; (1) at first, listen and read at the same time; (2) later, listen first, then read; and (3) finally, read first and check understanding by listening.

If you are an oral learner, you learn by talking aloud. There are not many learners of this type, but they do exist. In this case, you will want to be talking as much as possible. Recite dialogues, role plays, and poems to yourself whenever you can. When you are in the car or other appropriate venue, sing songs from the native culture.

Reading may be something that you do little of in your native language, and that makes development of reading skills even harder. Use the reading strategies in the previous section to help improve your reading skills.

podcasts + broadcasts = tools of auditory learners

Motor learners

Motor learners come in two varieties: mechanical and kinesthetic. Kinesthetic learner may be the label you have heard. Often, it is used to refer to both mechanical and kinesthetic learners, though kinesthetic learners use the large body muscles (legs, arms) for learning whereas mechanical learners use the small body muscles (fingers) for learning.

If you are a kinesthetic (large motor) learner, try to be active while listening and reading. March, jump, run, write, type. Whatever works… Just move! I had a very successful kinesthetic learner once who would try to remember new words by marching around his room and shouting them aloud. For him, an A+ student, it worked.

If you are a mechanical learner, write down everything as it comes up in class. Sure, you may never look at it again; many mechanical learners never do. They don't need to. Writing it down is enough to put it into their memory. I know that well because I am a mechanical learner. Write down anything you want to learn, for homework, for review, or just as you interact with native speakers. I am not learning a language at the moment, but I use the "jot it down" tactic for all kinds of things—and every once in a while I have to scoop up and trash a bunch of pieces of paper scraps where I have written down things that I have never looked at, never will look at, but whose content I have already stuffed into my memory.

If you are a mechanical learner, you may struggle with reading and listening. Strategies shared in the previous section of this book may help you with that struggle.

computers = tools of motor learners

Betty Lou Leaver Ph.D.

If new information comes at you in a non-preferred style, find the same information in a form that is more accessible to you!

Personality Types

Every person has a personality unlike any one else. However, there are some commonalities. Jung (1921/2016) identified four continua that he called personality types.[29] These are (1) extroversion-introversion, (2) intuiting-sensing, (3) thinking-feeling, and (4) rational-irrational.[30] One can also be situationally both one and the other, i.e. neither one end of a given continuum or the other.[31]

Extroversion _____ Introversion
Sensing _____ Intuiting
Thinking _____ Feeling
Rational (Judging) _____ Irrational (Perceiving)[32]

Extroverts and introverts

Jung does not use these terms in the way that the lay reader might expect. These terms do not mean gregarious

---

[29] Socionists (Filatova, 2009) and a mother-daughter team (Briggs-Myers and Myers, 1980) used Jung's continua to suggest 16 different styles. We will not cover all these styles here, but more information can be found in many sources, including *The Invisible Foreign Language Classroom* (Dabbs & Leaver, 2019) and *Achieving Success in Second Language Acquisition* (Leaver, Ehrman, & Shekhtman, 2002).

[30] Socionists and Jung use these terms, *rational* and *irrational*. Briggs-Myers and Myers (1980) use *judging* (*rational*) and *perceiving* (*irrational*).

[31] The Myers-Briggs Type Indicator (Briggs-Myers & Myers, 1980) can determine your personality type. If you do not already know it, you might find one of the websites that offers the test for free though the results can be less accurate than if you pay for the official MBTI.

[32] Remember, Jung called this continuum by the terms *rational* and *irrational*; MBTI uses the terms *judging* and *perceiving*. The MBTI terms are used in this section because they are the most commonly known.

or shy. Introverts can be gregarious, and extroverts can be shy. Rather, Jung defines the difference on the basis of energy and values. Extroverts gain energy when they are with others. Introverts lose energy when they are with others. Therefore, extroverts tend to be shallow processors, looking to others to join with in learning new information. Introverts tend to be deep processors and look only inside themselves in learning new information. Extroverts' values can be influenced by others. Introverts' values are set within, period.

As an extrovert, some of your best ways of going about gaining a foreign language are finding native speakers in your community to help and to get to know. Working with small groups will be comfortable for you, as will giving presentations (though the introverted nature of preparing a presentation of some in your smaller group might bore you). Chances are you will be better at expressing yourself orally in class than you will be on paper. (See if any of the writing strategies in the previous section of this book can help you with the latter.) In a class of mostly introverts, you might be perceived as loud, noisy, and perhaps even pushy. Be aware that can be the case, and "cool it" when you see that you are carrying the verbal activity for your whole class on your own shoulders.

As an introvert, some of your best ways of going about gaining a foreign language are reading and writing—and watching movies, especially if you are an auditory learner. If you feel a little overwhelmed when assigned to a small group, you could offer to be the recorder. For project presentations, rehearse, rehearse, and rehearse. Not only will it help get your nerves under control, it will also very much improve your speaking skills. Although it may feel uncomfortable, you will have to develop some willingness to speak up in class for two reasons: (1) you need the speaking practices, and (2) if the class has a lot of extroverts, you will not look passive, you will look unprepared and, unfairly, incompetent.

extrovert = stronger speaker skills
introvert = stronger reading and listening skills

Intuitives and sensers

Intuition and sensing differ in many important ways. This difference can be a strong bone of contention when working in groups—either on the job or in the classroom.

Intuitives are focused on possibilities, the future, and dreams. Facts and statistics bore them, and they usually will respond that statistics can be manipulated to show whatever the manipulator wants. They tend to prefer to learn inductively. If you are an intuitive, inductive learner, there is a fair chance that your textbook may be impeding your progress, as well as the structure of the course. Typically, textbooks are deductive tools. They teach the rules and then give opportunities to practice applying them. It is the practicing that causes the learning—for deductive learners. For intuitive learners, being able to figure out the rules on their own from lots of examples sets up the condition for learning. Learning is usually of the ah-hah/binding type once the rule is realized. Practice does not hut; it keeps it in memory. However, once bound, it is usually in memory, anyway. If you are an intuitive, inductive learner, you may need to take upon yourself setting up those conditions for learning/binding. One way to do that is to find a lot of authentic materials on the topic or that might contain the rule—the Internet can help with that. So, if you know your class will be starting to study past tense(s), then find a bunch of articles on history. Throw out those that are way beyond your level. Read as many of the others as you can within the time you have—before the past tense is introduced in your class and before you read your textbook. Once you think you have figured out what the past tense looks like, confirm by looking at your textbook or when the rules for formation and use are presented in the classroom.[33] (If you got it a bit wrong, your brain will usually make an automatic adjustment.)

Sensers are the polar opposite of the intuitives. Well, more accurately, strong sensers are the polar opposite of the strong intuitives. As you approach midpoint on the continuum, you are comfortable with traits from either pole. That said, sensers are focused on actualities, the present, and reality. Facts and statistics are meaningful to them, and they usually will use them to bolster, or even, form their opinions. They tend to prefer to learn deduc-

---

[33] Years ago, I went to Brazil for the first time. I knew Spanish but not a word of Portuguese. When I landed in São Paolo, I bought a book for learning Portuguese fast. It was called *Emotional Intelligence* and was a translation of Goleman's book by that title. Why that book and not a textbook? I had only a few days before I would be participating in a national education policy meeting which would be conducted in Portuguese. It worked. I was able to participate in the big group meeting and in the small group discussions. Sure, I was having to learn pronunciation on the spot and adjusting as I went along—and others had to work at times to understand me, but we got the work done. To answer the question, then, why that book, I offer the following explanations: (1) I could understand the book contents thanks to the fact that I knew the general content rather well; (2) I could figure out many of the words because of their similarity to Spanish words—they share an original language; and (3) the nature of the book provided all the tenses in a way to figure out which were which: descriptions were in the present tense, example stories were in the past tense, and suggestions for application of the theory were in the future tense. Not all books will serve as well, but raw, authentic material for intuitive learners can hurtle them past the beginning levels of study, especially if they have a chance to be learning the language in a country where it is spoken.

tively. Textbooks were written for them. Traditional classroom instruction was meant for them. Present a rule, explain it, practice it, use it. That is generally how they learn and remember. If you are a senser, chances are you will find yourself in a course that was prepared more or less with you in mind. However, not all courses are alike. Some courses, though, taught by intuitive teachers or those more in keeping with contemporary theories of teaching use authentic materials either in copious supplementation of a textbook or in lieu of one. In those cases, you may need to help yourself beyond the regular classroom assignments. How to do that? Work with a mentor or native speaker who can help you understand and practice the structure, words, and grammar of the text. Or, find a textbook that explains the same concepts in a way that better matches your need for deduction. Unlike the intuitives, it will probably not be helpful to try to do any of this in advance. Just be prepared once some linguistic phenomenon comes up in class that you do not understand to turn to whatever resources you have already identified.

intuitive = find answers yourself before class

deductive = let others guide you to the answers during or after class

Thinkers and feelers

Thinkers and feelers differ considerably in their basic values. This difference colors how they react to each other, other cultures, and the universe.

Thinkers put principle over people and choose justice over mercy. They are, by nature, logical. They tend to be book learners. The kinds of learning that will likely work best for you are reading books, getting your learning from books (authentic ones, written for native speakers, if you are an intuitive learner), and argumentation. Debates and competitions in the classroom will be helpful for you; if these are not on the menu for your course, then find other opportunities for these things, perhaps through language clubs, or how about putting together a debate club in your target language and pull in some other thinkers in your class. Equally important, if you are a thinker, you should be aware of some your likely expectations that might not be met in a course where the teacher is not a thinker. For example, your teacher might praise you in ways you think are overkill—and not even wait to take a look at how good your work is before gushing over your effort. The teacher means well; don't do what most thinkers do and become annoyed because you think the teacher is being condescending. More annoyingly, your teacher may want to know more about you than you want to share—realize that this is the nature of her personality; she cares.

Feelers put people over principle and choose mercy over justice. They are, by nature, compassionate. They tend to be book learners. The kinds of learning that will likely work best for you are those that involve interacting with people. If your course is all book work and reading, join a language club, and find native speakers in your community with whom you can develop a friendship or whom you can help in some way. Meet with other feelers in your class to work on homework, review, or otherwise work together. Equally important, if you are a feeler, you should be aware of some your likely expectations that might not be met in a course where the teacher is not a feeler. For example, your teacher might seem not to notice you—no praise for the effort you are making, maybe not seeming to call on you as often as others (could be a misperception), and seems cold to you. Check in with your feeling classmates. It is probably not you; they, too, probably have the same reaction to the teacher. Get past this sense of isolation from the teacher by realizing that a thinking teacher tends to be more interested in the brains of their students than in their personalities and their personal lives. So, keep in mind: it is not personal (pun intended)!

a collection of books = a likely thinker
a collection of people = a likely feeler

Judgers and perceiver

Judgers and perceivers differ in their need for closure. They also differ in their need for structure—or desire for freedom. And, they differ in whether or not they prefer to work on one thing or many things at the same time—though that correlation does not always hold up.

Judging is perhaps not the best term because judgers do not judge any more than anyone else does and are not any more judgmental than other people. They are judicious, sensible, detail-oriented learners. They put their work ahead of their play and feel at ease once they have closure (after making a purchase, after finishing homework, after finishing a test, etc.). If you are a judger, you can help yourself perform better by (1) clarifying your teacher's expectations, (2) not overscheduling yourself, (3) taking a deep breath and adapting to new expectations and changes in your environment, and (4) not rushing your work, which includes not turning in your exam as soon as you completed it but checking it over several times first.

Perceivers seem spontaneous, flexible, and sometimes fickle to judgers. They like their play, seem to have excess energy, and seem to always be open to new things, including activities that have been scheduled—oh, how they dislike schedules! Unlike judgers, who *finish* the assignment on the due date, all too often (for their own academic health) perceivers *begin* their assignments on the due date. Some perceivers have been heard to say, "Deadlines amuse me."[34] If you are a perceiver, here are some things that can help you fare better in your language (or any) course: (1) pay attention to deadlines—you might need to get some training in time-management skills, which would be well worth the effort; (2) when the structured environment is overwhelming, negotiate some flexibility if you can;[35] (3) keep your goal in front of you to keep yourself on track—post it on your refrigerator.

> *work now, play later = judger*
> *play now, work later = perceiver*

It takes all kinds to make the world go around, and you will find some of all of them in your language classrooms—be prepared to work together for everyone's sake.

---

[34] My husband is a perceiver who works as a graphic artist. At one copy shop where he worked, he had a sign on his computer that said, "Deadlines amuse me." I wonder how many customers it amused!

[35] I am a judger by day and a perceiver by night (i.e. in the middle of the continuum), and as a student I did get bored quite easily. I once negotiated with an English teacher to set my own writing assignments. Because I enjoyed my own self-assigned work, I ended up doing far more than the course required, delighting my teacher and enlightening me.

Cognitive Styles

A few cognitive styles have bee referred to and defined earlier (or footnoted). There are many kinds and systems of understanding cognition that have been proposed over the past 3-4 decades.

The one I use in this book is the E&L Cognitive Style Construct (Ehrman & Leaver, 2002; Leaver, 2019). I have chosen it principally because it encompasses many other systems—the reason it was designed: to simplify the proliferating models floating around academic programs.[36] For this book, it provides an easy overview of styles because the E&L subordinates ten subscales[37] to two overarching categories, which make it easier and simpler to use as a first-step instrument.

Cognition refers to the way people process information. After perceiving new information (through one or another sensory preference), a learner must process it, encoding it for memory. The effectiveness of how that is done depends on how strong the match is between a preferred cognitive style and the way the encoding occurs.

---

36 These other systems can be found in Kolb (2006), McCarthy (1987), Messick (1976), and elsewhere—an Internet search will bring up a treasure trove of them.

37 These subscales, not detailed in this book, can be found delineated in full in *The E&L Cognitive Style Construct: Supercharging Language Learning Success One Mind at a Time* (Leaver, 2019). The subscales are ten continua: inductive-deductive, random-sequential, field independent-field dependent, field sensitive-not field sensitive, impulsive-reflective, concrete-abstract, leveling-sharpening, synthetic-analytic, global-local, and analogue-digital. Some of the individual subscales can be exceptionally meaningful for specific languages (e.g., Arabic, with which almost all digital learners struggle), so becoming familiar with the subscales can be helpful.

The categories, like the MBTI categories, are a continuum. One can be situationally oriented and prefer one style under one set of circumstance and another under a different set. Most people, though, have a clear, either weak or strong, preference for one of the poles of the continuum.

The overarching categories of the E&L are called synopsis and ectasis, learners being either synoptic or ectenic. Their processes differ as do their pace of learning.

Synoptic learning

Synoptic learners learn though osmosis. They see phenomena as composites and do not consciously break down the language but acquire it through context via induction.

What happens to synoptic learners when they study languages?

At early stages of study, they move swiftly because the demand for accuracy is not high at early levels. Over time, though, they become "awfully fluent," with emphasis on the "awful" part, and often plateau just shy of the professional proficiency level because of an abundance of grammatical and lexical mistakes. The image I like to use for them is the hare, as in the tale of the hare and the tortoise, in which the hare gets way out ahead and then goes to sleep from boredom, and the tortoise wins. If you are a hare, flying through early stages of language learning, be aware of your tendency to over-guess and to approximate. Initially, you will be rewarded for that. Later, you will be punished when you have trouble getting up off your plateau.

How to take advantage of being a synoptic learner

If you are a synoptic learner, consider becoming acquainted early on with authentic materials. Regardless of how much or how little authentic material you use in your course, authentic materials are what will move you faster to your proficiency goal.

You can find newspapers and podcasts on the Internet, movies on Amazon, and books in the library. As for native speakers, you can find them in your community,[38] and if you don't have ready access to émigré groups, ask your teacher for an introduction.

Start watching movies even at lower levels of proficiency. Watch them over and over, understanding more each time. Watch them at the beginning of one month and re-watch them at the end of the next month. Congratulate yourself with how much more you understand after just two months. (Repeat as needed for self-confidence!)

You can also attend movies at a local theater if they are playing one in your target language. It will be a different experience since you can watch it only once (well, you could go back a few times, but that gets expensive). There you may have the added benefit of running into native speakers with whom you can discuss the movie.

Don't limit yourself to movies. Watch soap operas, interviews, game shows, news broadcasts—whatever else you can find.

Place some emphasis on interactive listening. Find ways to interact with native speakers on a continuing basis. Attend lectures with them, play music with them, help them with their needs, go where they go, and do what they

---

38 A synoptic graduate school friend of mine spent much of his grad school leisure time with Russian-speaking immigrants. Nearly immediately upon graduation, he got a job with Voice of America that is typically reserved for native speakers. He had known no Russian before the age of 18. His course brought him linguistic knowledge; his help to the émigré community brought him the help needed to develop near-native proficiency and get the job.

do. You will learn more than language from them; you will also learn their culture.[39]

As for reading, tie the topics to the content you are studying in your course, and you will get double the benefit for your efforts. Aim for extensive reading (a wide range of materials from a variety of different content areas), rather than intensive reading (deep reading of one text or a limited number of texts).[40] You will likely get a considerable amount of intensive reading experience in your course; doing more outside the classroom may be of less benefit to you than using the time you have to build breadth. As you reach higher levels of proficiency, you will need that breadth. If you are already an advanced learner, you might want to make yourself a reading list. In addition to novels and poetry, be sure to include a wide range of genres—and don't forget music.

---

39 When I, a strong synoptic who can nonetheless manage an ectasis-based course thanks to my linguistics background was in a basic Russian course, I joined the extracurricular orchestra led by two native-speaker instructors. Over time, I became quite good at playing the piccolo balalaika, a rare instrument. Both of these instructors belonged to a semi-professional Russian orchestra and, being in need of an instrument like the piccolo balalaika, invited me to join them. We rehearsed every Wednesday evening at one of their homes. I got to meet their families, join in professional discussions and kitchen talk, and no one ever spoke English to me. On Saturdays, we played gigs in the émigré community: weddings, parties, and other occasions. My language progressed in my course, but it surged as a result of my orchestra participation. When I got the highest score in my class, a remarkably near-perfect result on a proficiency test, I brought the test score to the orchestra director and told him, "This is the result of what you brought into my life."

40 In extensive reading, you read for information and content; you pick up the structure intuitively. In intensive reading, you begin with structure and build meaning, based on the structure, finishing by understanding the content.

see the forest, miss the trees = synoptic learners

Ectenic learning

Ectenic learners learn though a deliberate pulling apart of the language; they see matter as built of parts and go about learning consciously, analyzing the language deductively, even preferring decontextualization.

What happens to ectenic learners when they study languages?

At early stages of study, they struggle as a sea of authentic language overwhelms their need for details and accuracy. While the course may not demand accuracy at lower levels, ectenic learners do, and they continue some time in a "painfully accurate" manner, with emphasis on the "painful" part. They do not sail onto a high plateau like the synoptics; rather, they step up onto one small plateau after another as they inch forward in proficiency. The image I like to use for them is the tortoise; they keep going, one painful step at a time—and win the race. Among very high achievers, those who reach near-native levels of proficiency, in my experience and research, the tortoises (ectenics) are over-represented.[41] That may be explained by the fact that at the higher proficiency levels, greater accuracy is required.

How to take advantage of being an ectenic learner

If you are an ectenic learner, authentic materials, whether handled judiciously in the classroom with lots of support or met in the wild, are likely to overwhelm you, leaving you flustered, likely frustrated, not knowing where to start. Certainly, you will need to prepare in advance

---

[41] If you are interested in that research, check out Leaver (1986) and Leaver and Shekhtman (2002).

if you want to hold your own in the classroom and meet teacher expectations.

If you know you will be watching a movie in class, see if you can find that movie ahead of time and watch it at home. Try to get the script for the movie and read that in advance, breaking down the language as you would for a reading text. Analyze the script until you are sure you understand the general plot and the characters, looking up words, expressions, grammar—whatever structural help you need. Do not expect to understand every word; that is not necessary. Understand enough to be able to follow the plot when watching the movie, which will be easier with the visual props. Read a synopsis of the movie and a review of it. Get to know everything you can about the movie before you watch it. If you are watching it at home on DVD, watch it in segments, replaying as needed to follow the plot. You will probably not be able to understand every word, and do not try to. That may annoy you, but really, you do not pay attention to or hear every word when you watch a movie in your native language. If you prepare in this way, you will feel much more comfortable watching the movie in class. Go to class prepared with notes, listing the right expressions, that you can use to discuss the movies. Don't stop there, though. After the movie is shown in class, watch it again at home—all the way through without stopping and see how much more you understand. Do that again in two months; it will increase your comfort and confidence.

You can prepare to meet with native speakers in the same way. Determine what you will be talking about—just some chit-chat, an event you will be attending together, or some area in which you will be providing assistance. You can put together preparatory notes with the kinds of expressions you think you will need to accomplish your goal in meeting with the native speaker(s)—though you will probably not want to pull them out in front of people![42]

To prepare for authentic reading in class, look through the text at home in advance if you have that opportunity. If you cannot read through it easily and understand it from a first reading, then go after the text structurally. Break the sentences into their key parts: subject, action, receiver of the action, adding details once you understand the skeleton. If there are words that you do not know, try to figure them out by breaking them apart or context. While the latter tactic is not your forte, it is a good capability to build. Then, break the text into paragraphs—think about what each paragraph adds to the message and why it is there. Finally, outline the text as if you were an author preparing to write it. After all that, read through the text again. Now, do you understand it completely? With time, a general increase in proficiency, and repetition of this approach, you will find that you are able to read many articles through, understanding them the first time, like you do in your native language. As an ectenic learner, you just have to build up to it.

see the trees, miss the forest = ectenic learner

---

[42] When I taught Russian, I would assign individual projects in which my students were to help native speakers with specific needs. I would meet with the students in advance to ensure that they had control of the basic language they would need for the task. Once, a young lady was going to take a pregnant native speaker to the doctor. We went over obstetrical terms relating to pregnancy and childbirth. My student was ready! Except, as it turns out, the woman was not pregnant and was going to the doctor for a D&C! With some of the basic medical terminology she had learned, my student managed to get through the doctor's appointment without too much psychological scarring! In fact, she went on to help other immigrants, major in Russian, and become a professional interpreter.

Betty Lou Leaver Ph.D.

Both synopsis and ectasis are needed in language learning. Take advantage of which style is your preference and, over time, deliberately build skills that help manage tasks of the opposite type.

Doing Well on Tests

Betty Lou Leaver Ph.D.

If it were up to me, I would never give a test. As a teacher, I have never found that a test provided much useful information beyond what I already knew from interacting with learners—and they certainly traumatize some learners. As a program administrator, I was in the position for three different programs I oversaw not to require tests. I did not, and learners learned and, in my opinion, faster because they were not spending time studying for tests and taking tests but rather learning the language.[43]

That said, tests are very likely here to stay. They are even big business for testing companies. So, clearly nearly every learner will need to be able to deal well with in-class and course tests and general proficiency tests used for a variety or purposes other than course grades.

I would urge all readers of this book to focus first on language learning. In that way, you will also be prepared for a test. If you focus on test results and test preparation, you may get a good grade but not reach your language goals, including those needed for a dream job. If you have the language, a few strategies will help you do well on nearly any test. Those are discussed in this section of this book.

---

43 I did do diagnostic assessment, which is formative proficiency testing, meaning that grades are not given and the purpose is to determine what has been acquired and what more, specifically, needs to be acquired to reach the next higher level of proficiency.

Betty Lou Leaver Ph.D.

Classroom Tests

The better you know the language, the better you will do on the test. Period. It does not really matter what type of test it is.

Classroom tests can take many different forms. Most, though, will usually fit into one of three types of tests: achievement, prochievement (pro-achievement), or proficiency. Each has a format; each has a content. These differ somewhat among the test types.

Achievement tests

Achievement tests are a check of your knowledge. They may try also to test your language skills, but generally that can only be accomplished by a proficiency test.

Format of achievement tests

The format of an achievement test takes a limited number of forms. Sometimes the forms are combined. The test might have multiple-choice answers, fill-ins, or matching items. Sometimes, they will have questions requiring short answers, but all the short answers must be the same. In all its forms, an achievement test allows for only one right answer.[44]

Test content

Think about taking the SAT or GRE. You can do scads of practice tests, but unless you know the mathematics upon which the test is based and have a broad English vo-

---

[44] Sometimes, you may get a multiple-choice test that looks like it has more than one right answer because one or more questions ask you to indicate "all that apply" or "all that are correct." That is still a test with one right answer. You have to pick "all" of the items correctly.

cabulary so that you know the words on the test, you won't test well. Practice tests may help you be more comfortable with a test format, but they won't give you the knowledge you need to excel on the SAT or GRE. To do well, you actually have to acquire a solid knowledge of math and English. Likewise, to do well on any test, including an achievement test, you must have studied and learned the content on which the test is based.

Achievement tests will always be based on the material (including authentic materials) that have been presented in class or in your textbook. Review all of that material—early, not the night before the test. In fact, it is always wise, in order to keep your working memory working well, to review both new and older materials periodically.

Improving your performance

If you do not do well on achievement tests, you can practice eliminating your problems. Check out some of the biggest problems for some learners and what to do about them:

- Most of these tests are timed, and you may need to practice hurrying up.[45] Filling in the circle or bar that is beside the right answer very carefully and perfectly will not get you a better test score. It will

---

[45] When she was in high school, my daughter gained almost 200 points on her PSAT by doing this. After she did poorly when she first took the test while the print-out of the results showed she had answered only the first half of the questions (all of those correctly), I knew her reflective learning style was causing the problem. Although the school thought she should enroll in an expensive test preparation course, I knew content was not the problem. Her reflectivity was. I brought home 50 or so bubble forms with demographic information to be filled in (name, address, etc.), and made her fill them out faster and faster. When she could get a form filled out in less than a minute, she signed up to take the PSAT again—and her results soared.

slow you down. You will not finish. Your unanswered questions will count against you. It does not matter whether you know the answers or not because you did not finish the test to show anyone that you do. This is not a content issue, so practice filling out test forms faster.

- Multiple-choice answers leave a lot of room for creative learners (the intuitive types) to find a reason for every answer to be correct. Don't overthink it; answer what seems would be the most traditional or common response.

- Review your test for possible slip-ups, but where you are not sure, don't talk yourself out of your first answer when you review. Generally, the first answer (your natural instinct) is the correct one.

*studied texts + studied topics
+ one right answer = achievement test*

Prochievement tests

Prochievement tests are sometimes called pro-achievement tests because they include both proficiency and achievement components. As such, they propose to check both your knowledge and your language skills.

Format of prochievement tests

Prochievement tests may look a lot like achievement tests. They may ask you to answer multiple-choice questions or fill out charts—any of the formats that you have come to expect with an achievement. There may be a separate section based on an authentic listening or reading text or both with some open-ended answers. Or, the authentic text might be followed by multiple choice or other kinds of achievement-test questions.

Test content

The authentic texts on a pro-achievement test may, probably will, be new to you. This is how your language skills are being tested. Can you transfer skills you have developed through the study of other texts to new ones? If you can only read texts you have already studied, chances are you are pulling from memory and not applying language skills. These authentic texts, however, will not usually take a "gotcha" form. The topics of the texts will be the same topics that you have studied in your course.

Improving your performance

If you do not do well on prochievement tests, you can work on improving your performance. Here are some of the ways you can do that:

- Use the suggestions provided for achievement tests to improve your performance on the proficiency component of the prochievement test.

- Prepare to handle new, unknown texts by reading and listening to as many texts as you can find and have time to work with that are on the same topic as the texts you are reading in the course. You can find them online, in the library, from your teacher—you know the sources.

- Work on improving your reading and listening strategies as suggested in the section of this book on strategies and tactics.

- You cannot cram for the proficiency component of this test. More than for a knowledge test, cramming for a proficiency test is useless. You must have already built up the language skills you need well before you need them. So, read something extra on the topic you are reading about in class every day or every other day. Also, every day or every other day, listen to a podcast, YouTube, movie, television program, or news broadcast on one of the topics you are studying in the classroom.

*new texts + studied topics
+ varied right answers = prochievement test*

Proficiency tests

Proficiency tests focus exclusively on checking your language skills. How well do you read, write, listen, or speak? That is what a proficiency test sets out to find out, whether it is a summative test that gives you a grade or a formative test that provides suggestions on how to improve your skills.

Format of prochievement tests

Classroom proficiency tests can take a multiple-choice or other one-right answer format, but they usually do not. Typically, they will ask you open-ended questions. You may get graded on how well your write as well as what you write. They may also give you a task to do: fill out a chart, make a schedule, and the like—which you will not be able to do if you do not understand what you hear or read.

Test content

The test content of a proficiency test is generally a collection of authentic materials. Some of these materials may reflect the topics you have studied in class; others may not. Remember, the test is not looking for your depth of knowledge but for the level of development of your skill set in one or more of the four skills: reading, writing, listening, and/or speaking.

Improving your performance

If you do not do well on proficiency tests, you can work on improving your performance. Here are some of the ways you can do that:

- As with prochievement tests, prepare to handle new, unknown texts by reading and listening to as many texts as you can find and have time to work with that are on the same topic as the texts you are using in the course.
- Work on improving your reading and listening strategies as suggested in the section of this book on strategies and tactics.
- Remember that you cannot cram for a proficiency test, so read, listen, write, and speak as much as you can every day both on your classroom and textbook topics and, stretching, on other topics that interest you.
- Don't spend your learning time throughout the course focused on getting a good score on any one test. It is counterproductive. Focus on learning the language, and the test score will take care of itself.
- Proficiency tests can inspire anxiety. After all, it is natural to fear, or at least be nervous about, the unknown, and likely not enough is known going into a proficiency test that can make you completely comfortable. Try some of these tips for dealing with text anxiety:
    - Eat well regularly, and before the test remember your banana and carbs—and forget your caffeine

and candy bar.
- Sleep well all week but especially the night before the test so that your brain can be re-energized to work on all thrusters.
- Use some positive self-talk: tell yourself that you can handle the test—and mean it.
- Pump up your self-esteem: think about all the times you have done well, especially when you have done well on testes.
- Develop a positive attitude toward the test and look forward to showing what you know.
- If you are nervous about the test, get there early; it is a good idea to get there early, whether you are nervous or not; getting there late will add to your nervousness.
- If you feel anxiety as you begin the test, read through the questions quickly, answer the easiest first, and then go on.
- If you feel anxiety during the test, close your eyes briefly, take a deep breath, and then go on.
- If you experience debilitating anxiety before all tests, not just language tests, you might want to consult an expert.

new texts + new topics
+ varied right answers = proficiency test

Nearly every day, read, write, listen, and/or speak on the topics you are studying, and the test will be a breeze.

Betty Lou Leaver Ph.D.

Written General Proficiency Test

Sometimes language learners have to take a general proficiency test not connected with any course they are take. These tests differ from classroom proficiency tests. They are broader in scope and more demanding in the skill set they expect. There are very few such tests in existence. The American Council on Teaching Foreign Languages developed one for academic programs (K-12 and university); you can find information at the organization's website. The Foreign Service Institute has its own proficiency test for diplomats (contents not publicly available), and the US Department of Defense administers the Defense Language Proficiency Test (DLPT) to its departmental employees, service members, and employees of other government agencies; DLPT information can be found online at many sites, including in the English Wikipedia. Some other government agencies also have their own proficiency tests, but that information is not available to the general public.

Preparing for the test

Here are some thoughts to keep in mind as soon as you know you will be taking a general proficiency test:

- We become good at what we practice. If you spend a lot of time trying to guess what will be on a proficiency test and practicing its format,[46] you lose a lot of language-learning time, and that will not serve you well on the test.

- Proficiency tests of any sort are looking at how well

---

46 If the test will be in a format with which you are unfamiliar, then it does make sense to practice that format a few times. The operant word is *few*. Once you are comfortable with the format, stop. Go back to spending your time on learning more language.

you handle the language; for that, you need good skills, which are built up over time, not overnight. To gain these skills:

- Develop good reading, writing, listening, and speaking strategies.
- Read everything you can get your hands on. Do not discriminate by genre.[47] Read chat, newsletters, blogs, history, sociology, novels, poems, memoirs, essays, notes, letters, comic books; if it is written and you can get your hands on it, read it. Prioritize your reading toward authentic materials of any sort.
- Listen to everything you can, preferably authentic materials such as movies, YouTube, television (Oh, my, the range of topics, formats, and levels of language that provides!),[48] and anything else you can find. Is it over your head? Fine. If you listen enough, it won't be over your head for long.
- Speak with everyone you can—even if it is hard.
- Write in various genres and share your writing with a native speaker; ask for correction.

---

47 One of the best language learners I know, a colleague from Germany with English skills that are every bit as good as any educated native speaker of English claims that she built her language skills through "promiscuous reading"—never saw a story, book, or text that she was not willing to read, including comic books and notes native speakers wrote to each other.

48 When my then 11-year-old daughter and I spent part of a year in Moscow, she learned Russian initially by watching Winnie the Pooh cartoons. The language was way over her head, but she knew the content and so understood quickly. Of course, going to a Moscow school every day also put her in over her head, but again very quickly she began interacting with the school children in her class. So, don't back off from the hard stuff.

- As you read, write, listen, and speak, try to increase the number of learning strategies you use. A great starting place is the Strategy Inventory for Language Learning (Oxford, 1986).[49]
- Authentic materials do not occur without a context. Learn the context you will need to understand what you are reading and hearing: become familiar with the culture(s) where your target language is spoken.
- Once you develop some language skills, start tutoring others. The best way to learn something is to teach it. Teach your tutorees content, but also teach them learning strategies for skill development. Everything you teach others will reinforce what you know and what you can do.

daily preparation = better test scores

Taking the test

If you use all four skills[50] on a regular basis, when you get to the test, you will be prepared. Now, here are some suggestions for handling the test:

- Follow the suggestions in the previous section for classroom proficiency test taking and anxiety relief.
- When you do not understand what you are reading

---

49 This is the original SILL. Oxford has updated it over the years; check out her books on learning strategies—they are a rich source for what you need.

50 Even if you will be tested on only listening and reading, you will fare less well on the test than someone who has used all four skills. Research (Hopman & McDonald, 2018; Hsu, 2004; Leaver & Shekhtman, 2003, among a fair number of other studies) has shown that these skills reinforce each other—and you need as much reinforcement as you can get!

or hearing—be prepared that there will be much that you do not understand so don't let that panic you but rather:

- focus on what you do understand and use your reading and listening strategies to figure out as much about what you do not;
- skip the question—it is better to get one question wrong than to lose so much time on one question that you will not have time to finish ten (if points are not taken off for a wrong answer, make a quick guess—you may be right—and go on);
- pull in background knowledge and eliminate some of the answers as incorrect simply because they do not reflect reality or the culture, then choose the remaining one that seems closest to what you do understand and go on; and
- pull in content knowledge to give a context to what you are reading or hearing.

* Read carefully; avoid careless mistakes.
* Concentrate on the paper in front of you; it is easy to get distracted by people around you or noises inside or outside of the room so try to get into "the flow" and be aware of only yourself and the test.
* If the test is timed, pace yourself.

daily preparation + informed test taking = best test scores

Learn the language in all its forms to do well on a proficiency test.

Oral Proficiency Interview (OPI)

All of the organizations that administer written proficiency tests also administer oral proficiency tests. You can find information at the same sites as given for the written tests. Please note that Language Testing International (LTI) administers the OPI of the American Council on Teaching Foreign Languages (ACTFL) so LTI's site is the best place to go for information. Some private institutes, organizations, and companies have developed various forms of an OPI, but they are not as commonly known or used as those of ACTFL and the US government.

Preparing for the test

Here are some thoughts to keep in mind as soon as you know you will be taking an OPI:

- Given that we become good at what we practice (and not good at what we do not), then it goes without saying that we should practice speaking as much as possible, including
  - with the teacher in class;
  - with classmates in class, during breaks, and outside class (make an agreement to speak only the target language to each other);
  - with native speakers wherever you can find them; and
  - to yourself when no one else is available.
- Speaking about talking to yourself, don't overlook that as a possible way to rehearse for an OPI; think about what topics might come up or what tasks you might be asked to do and then play the roles of both you and the interviewer—if you guess any of these

correctly, you comfort level will dramatically increase during the interview.
- Read a lot; the majority of near-native speakers report that they achieved their speaking skills as a result of copious reading.[51]
- OPI formats differ, depending upon who is giving the OPI; find out details well in advance so that you know how to orient your preparation (e.g., if you are going to have to deliver a monologue, which is not a normal part of every day speech, you may want to practice doing a few of those, especially if your course does not include giving presentations as part of its instructional program).
- If you read no other book than this one, read *How to Improve Your Foreign Language Immediately* (Shekhtman, 2013; it contains seven tools that will help you for any time you need to speak, including during an OPI.

*reading + speaking + immersion
in the language = ready to take an OPI*

Taking the OPI

An OPI, regardless of who does it, has some type of warm up (or period of getting acquainted), questions at your comfort level, questions above your comfort level, and for some versions, a brief formal closure or winding down. Depending upon the organization giving the OPI,

---

[51] Leaver and Atwell, as reported in Leaver and Shekhtman (2003) interviewed over 100 learners of foreign languages who had achieved near-native levels of proficiency in their foreign language; more than 80% reported the positive influence of extensive reading on their speaking skills.

you might be expected to answer questions, act as an interpreter, give a briefing, or accomplish specific tasks.

Here are some tips for handing the range of communications that may be required of you:

- Come to the OPI early, rested, and having eaten properly.
- Relax. Yes, that is easier said than done, but if you cannot, your interactions will not be at their best. Follow some of the suggestions for test anxiety given for classroom tests to help calm yourself.
- Adopt an attitude of curiosity; you will be meeting someone as the interviewer, and the test is something new—it may be fun.
- Generally, a lot of questions will be about topics that you could be expected to know and probably do know; speak up and show what you know.
- Try to be accurate, but don't obsess over grammar; either you have already internalized the forms or you have not.
- Listen carefully to the questions. If you don't understand the question, ask for clarification. You cannot answer a question you do not understand.
- If you don't know a word or expression you need, paraphrase—you should already have had a lot of practice in doing this.
- If you don't know much about a topic that is brought up, just say so.
- Don't try to buffalo the interviewer; this is one test where you cannot guess, and interviewers are well trained to ferret out everything you know and don't know.

- And, in spite of what you may hear people say about alcohol helping people to speak another language more fluently, don't touch the stuff! You want clear speech, not slurred speech on your test.

good preparation + attitude of curiosity = more comfortable test + more accurate results

Conclusion:
Learning Languages in a Hurry

Betty Lou Leaver Ph.D.

I have often been in a situation where I have either had to learn a language in a hurry, sometimes in just a few days or weeks, or teach in a language a hurry, in just a few weeks. I believe that the advice contained in the previous pages will help you learn your foreign language faster, better, and with more enjoyment.

The most important thing to remember in choosing what to use from this book is who you are. Know what you want from your language learning experience. Know how, when, where, and with whom you learn best. Know your strengths and your weaknesses, and work to improve both.

Most of all know that there will be challenges along the way. The very best advice I can give you is to rise to them. Don't let anyone overwhelm you. Most of all, don't let them think that you cannot be a good language learner. Keep your self-esteem high, whatever that takes, and you will find that you have a positive attitude—and that positive attitude, with some strategies and tactics, will take you a long way.

Good luck!

Betty Lou Leaver Ph.D.

References & Resources

Barsch, J. (1996). *Barsch Learning Style Inventory.* Novato, CA: Academic Therapy Publications.

Bassham, L. (2011). *With winning in mind.* The Mentashowini Management System.

Beck, A. (1979). *Cognitive therapy and the emotional disorders.* London: Plume.

Briggs-Myers, I., & Myers, P. (1980). *Gifts differing.* Palo Alto, CA: Consulting Psychologists Press.

Brown, H. D. (2007). *Principles of language learning and teaching.* White Plains, NY: Pearson Education.

Brown, J. S., Collins, A., Duguid, S. (1989). Situated cognition and the culture of learning. *Educational Researcher* 18 (1): 32-42.

Budner, S. (1962). Intolerance of ambiguity as a personality variable. *Journal of Personality, 30,* 29-50.

Burdick, E., & Lederer, W. (1958/2019). *The ugly American.* New York: W. W. Norton.

Coalition of Distinguished Language Centers. (2015). *What works: Helping students reach near-native second-language competence.* Virginia Beach, VA: Villa Magna LLC.

Corin, A., & Leaver, B. L. (2019). *Fields of the mind: History, theory, and application of cognitive field concepts to language learning.* Hollister, CA: MSI Press, LLC.

Craik, F. I. M., & Lockhart, R. S. (1972). *Levels of processing: A framework for memory research. Journal of Verbal Learning and Verbal Behavior* 11: 671-684.

Dabbs, L., & Leaver, B. L. (2019). *The invisible classroom: Bringing hidden dynamics to light for individual and group harmony and success.* Hollister, CA: MSI Press, LLC.

Ehrman, M. E., & Leaver, B. L. (2002). *The E&L Cognitive Styles Construct.* Unpublished, copyrighted, and registered instrument.

Duke. S. T. (2014). *Preparing to study abroad; Learning to cross cultures.* Sterling, VA: Stylus Publishing

Ehrman, M. E., & Leaver, B. L. (2003). Cognitive styles in the service of language learning. *System* 31 (3): 393-415.

Ehrman, M. E., & Leaver, B. L. (2002). *The E&L Cognitive Styles Construct.* Unpublished, copyrighted, and registered instrument.

Ehrman, M. E., Leaver, B. L. & Oxford, R. L. (2003). A brief overview of individual differences in second language learning. *System* 31 (3): 313- 330.

Filatova, E. (2009). *Understanding the people around you.* Hollister, CA: MSI Press.

Griffiths, C. (2008). *Lessons from good language learners.* Cambridge, UK: Cambridge University Press.

Hartmann, E. (1991). *Boundaries in the mind.* New York: Basic Books.

Hopman, E. W. M., & McDonald, M. C. (2018), Production practice during language learning improves comprehension. *Psychological Science* 29 (6): 961-971.

Hsu, J. (2004). *Reading, writing, and reading-writing in the secondary language classroom: A balanced curriculum.* ERIC Document downloaded from the Internet: https://files.eric.ed.gov/fulltext/ED492895.pdf.

Jung, C. (1921/2016). *Psychological types.* (Reissue of *Psychologischen Typen*). London: Routledge.

Kolb, D. (2006). *Organizational behavior: An experiential approach.* New York: Pearson.

Leaver, B. L. (2019). *The E & L Cognitive Styles Construct: Supercharging language learning success one mind at a time.* Hollister, CA: MSI Press, LLC.

Leaver, B. L. (1997). *Teaching the whole class.* Thousand Oaks, CA: Corwin Press.

Leaver, B. L. (1986). Hemisphericity of the brain and foreign language teaching. *Folia Slavica* 8:76-90.

Leaver, B. L., Dubinsky, I., & Champine, M. (2004). *Passport to the world: Learning to communicate in a foreign language.* San Diego, CA: LARC Press.

Leaver, B. L., Ehrman, M. E., & Shekhtman, B. S. (2002.) *Achieving success in second-language acquisition.* Cambridge, UK: Cambridge University Press.

McCarthy, B. (1987). The 4-Mat System: Teaching to learning styles with right/left mode techniques. Barrington, IL: EXCEL.

Messick, S. (1976). *Individuality in learning.* San Francisco: Jossey-Bass Publishers.

Morrison, T., & Conaway, W. A. (2006). *Kiss, bow, or shake hands: The bestselling guide to doing business in 60 countries.* Avon, MA: Adams Media.

Ortman, D. (2015). *Anxiety anonymous: The big book on anxiety addiction.* Hollister, CA: MSI Press.

Oxford, R. (1986). *Development and psychometric testing of the Strategy Inventory for Language Learning.*

Arlington, VA: US Army Research Institute for the Behavioral and Social Sciences.

Oxford, R. (2017). *Teaching and researching language learning strategies: Self-regulation in context.* London: Routledge.

Oxford, R., Ehrman, M. & Lavine, R. (1991). Style wars: Teacher-student style conflicts in the language classroom. In Magnan, S. S. (ed.), *Challenges in the 1990s for college foreign language programs* (pp. 1–25). Boston: Heinle & Heinle.

Patrick, G. (1989). *Roots of the Russian language: An elementary guide to wordbuilding.* Lincolnwood, IL: National Textbook Company.

Piaget, J., & Inhelder, B. (1971/2015). *Memory and intelligence.* (Psychology Revivals). East Sussex, UK: Psychology Press.

Reeves, L. (2019). Good language learners demystified: A look at the qualities that make them successful. Downloaded from the Internet: https://www.fluentu.com/blog/good-language-learner/

Rowan, K. (2011). Quitting smoking improves memory. *My Health News Daily.* Downloaded from https://www.livescience.com/16144-quitting-smoking-improves-memory.html.

Rubin, J., & Thompson, I. (1994). *How to be a more successful language learner.* Boston, MA: Cengage.

Ryding, K. (2005). *A reference grammar of Arabic.* Cambridge, UK: Cambridge University Press.

Shekhtman, B.S. (2013). *How to improve your foreign language immediately.* Virginia Beach, VA: Villa Magna LLC.

Stevick, E. (1996). *Memory, meaning, and method: Some psychological perspectives on language learning.* Boston: Heinle.

Stevick. E. (1990). *Success with foreign languages: Seven Who Achieved It and What Worked for Them.* Upper Saddle River, NJ: Prentice Hall.

Thagard, P., & Aubie, B. (2008). Emotional consciousness: A neural model of how cognitive appraisal and somatic perception interact to produce qualitative experience. *Consciousness and Cognition* 17: 8311-834.

Thagard, P., & Stewart, T. C. (2010). The AHA! Experience: Creativity through emergent binding in neural networks. *Cognitive Science.* Downloaded from https://onlinelibrary.wiley.com/doi/full/10.1111/j.1551-6709.2010.01142.x.

Townsend, C., & Komar, E. S. (2000). *Czech through Russian.* Bloomington, IN: Slavica Publishers.

Vygotsky, L. S. (1978). *Mind in society: The development of higher psychological processes.* Boston, MA: Harvard University Press.

Wenden. A. (1991). *Learner strategies for learner autonomy: Planning and implementing learner training for language learners.* Upper Saddle River, NJ: Prentice Hall.

Betty Lou Leaver Ph.D.

MSI Language & Culture Books

Currently available:

Living in Blue Sky Mind: Basic Buddhist Teachings for a Happy Life (Diedrichs)

Road to Damascus (E. Imady)

Syrian Folktales (M. Imady)

The Invisible Foreign Language Classroom (Dabbs & Leaver)

The Rise and Fall of Muslim Civil Society (O. Imady)

The Subversive Utopia: Louis Kahn and the Question of National Jewish Style in Jerusalem (Sakr)

Think Yourself into Becoming a Language Learner Super Star (Leaver)

Thoughts without a Title [views from the Middle East] (Henderson)

When You're Shoved from the Right, Look to Your Left (O. Imady)

Forthcoming in 2019

Fields of the Mind (Corin & Leaver)

Managing Cognitive Distortions & Mitigating Affective Dissonance (Salyer & Leaver)

The E&L Construct: Supercharging Language Learning Success One Mind at a Time (Leaver)

Planned for 2020

Arabic in a Hurry (Farraj)

Damascus amid the War (M. Imady)

English in a Hurry (Cleret)

For Love of the Chidlren of Colombia (Fr. Julio Juarin de Sosa)

Russian in a Hurry (Suhkovetchenko)

Building a Life from Foreign Parts (Leaver)

MSI Related Books

Currently available:
Understanding the Analyst (Quinelle)
Understanding the Critic (Quinelle)
Understanding the Entrepreneur (Quinelle)
Understanding the People around You (Filatova)
Understanding the Seeker (Quinelle)

Forthcoming in 2019
Understanding the Performer (Quinelle)
Understanding the Professional (Quinelle)

Planned for 2020
I Am, You Are, My Kid Is (Leaver)
Understanding the Craftsman (Quinelle)
Understanding the Romantic (Quinelle)

CPSIA information can be obtained
at www.ICGtesting.com
Printed in the USA
FSHW021648250919
62385FS